ACKN

The writers wish to ⟨…⟩ producers and preser⟨…⟩ the BBC and inde⟨…⟩ allowed their telephone lines to be opened up for phone-in programmes on the subject of OOBE's (out-of-body experiences). Because this was a somewhat off-beat subject, many of them were a little sceptical to start with, but it is fair to state that in every case, without exception, the reaction from the general public was so staggering that even the most doubtful of presenters were forced to concede that.. "there must be something in it".

We would like to thank the many members of the clergy who gave us their time and assistance in finding modern day miracles. In particular, we extend our thanks to the Rt. Revd. Graham St.John-Willey, B.Sc.(Hons), also to Rev. Philip J. Kerr, Prof. of Dogmatic Theology, Gillis College, Edinburgh. A very special word of appreciation is due to Father Keith Sawyer M.A. for his endless patience and kindness.

In their various ways the following people have been invaluable to us in preparing the book: Sheila Bone, Kirsty Tomkins, Joe O'Reilly, Andrew Sutton, Nigel Davis, Derek Schroder, Roger Deller and Justin Massie-Taylor.

It would not have been possible to write this book without the co-operation of all the people who took the time and trouble to share their mystic experiences with us. To these people we are forever grateful.

A Sinclair Book

First published in Great Britain in 1989
by Sinclair Publishing Ltd.

Typeset by Metropress (Type) Ltd, Wellingborough
Printed and bound in Great Britain by
Cox & Wyman Ltd, Reading

BRITISH LIBRARY CATALOGUING IN
PUBLICATION DATA

Harrison, Peter
  Mystic Forces
  1. Mysticism
  I. Title   II Harrison, Mary
  149'.3

  ISBN 1-872149-00-6

Sinclair Publishing Ltd.,
50 Oxford Street, Wellingborough,
Northants., NN8 4JH, U.K.

MYSTIC FORCES

BY
PETER & MARY HARRISON

FOREWORD

Over the past five years or so, since the publication of our book *Life Before Birth*, we have received a steady flow of correspondence from people all over the country, reporting their stories of the unexplained, unusual or prophetic dreams, apparitions, hauntings, miracles, faith healing, fateful encounters and other inexplicable experiences. Some of the stories are sad, some funny, some, on further probing, can possibly be explained by rational means, some are probably due to wishful thinking.

In this book we are looking at true stories of out-of-the-body experiences (OOBEs). These have been selected from over three thousand case histories of ordinary people in everyday situations finding themselves released from their physical bodies. They float in a state of suspension from where they can look down upon their physical bodies, all the thinking/feeling personality being contained in the released entity, soul, spirit, call it what you will.

In some cases, the people have been in traumatic situations, such as on a hospital operating table or in a car crash, but the vast majority of people report that they had the experience in normal circumstances, without any warning whatsoever. Many of them were so disorientated that they could hardly believe what was happening to them. All of them are adamant that they were most definitely NOT having a dream. Most of them state that they had never heard of out-of-the-body experiences before it happened to them, and it was only afterwards that they started to ask questions in order to find out more.

It appears that the phenomenon is fairly widespread and is not confined to any particular type of person. We have cases from a complete cross-section of the public, every creed, colour and social background, and from all age groups. The only common denominator seems to be the hesitancy to speak about the subject, for fear of being ridiculed. Many people are terrified by the experiences, and just as many find profound joy and peace. All of them state that they are not afraid of death because they know that the spirit exists independently of the physical body.

All of the people in this book have experienced spontaneous release, not drug-induced, with the exception of the controlled hospital operation cases. We reject all cases where controlled methods of achieving out-of-the-body experience have been instigated. We are aware that some people practise a formula for achieving OOBEs. We are strongly against such procedures. We believe that if, and when, a person is meant to experience the spirit leaving the body it will happen to them when the time is right.

Peter and Mary Harrison
Easter, 1989

CONTENTS

INTRODUCTION

Some of the stories related in this book are quite remarkable; some perhaps have no reasonable explanation, and indeed there may be some which have resulted from head injuries, as Dr Fenwick's paper suggested in 1985. Some may be the result of delusions or plain error, but the vast majority ring true in some way. There are some which I can personally vouch for, either because I was involved, or present, or because I know the people involved.

In January 1977, whilst at college, I suffered a mild heart attack. Fellow students carried me to my rooms and put me into bed. They summoned assistance from the medical staff and, at the same time, called out the Chaplain, a local Methodist Minister, The Rev. Stephen Beer, M.A., S.T.M. I cannot recall who arrived first on the scene, but alongside Stephen came another student, Alison Richards, who was a resident in that household. It was in the early hours of the morning, and it was very dark and cold outside. My college room seemed dimly lit. I cannot recall the doctor or the nurse examining me, but all at once I found 'myself' apparently out of my body, looking down on the study bedroom from what seemed to be ceiling height. 'I' was still lying on the bed, Alison kneeling on the floor beside me. The doctor and Stephen were turned away from the still body and a few paces from the feet and yet, from 'my' new vantage point, I could see their faces and I overheard their quiet, concerned conversation.

I felt a great sense of peace. Above and behind me were not the solid ceiling and walls of the building, but what seemed to be a gentle, all-pervading, golden light. I remember being very calm and in no pain or distress, in distinct contrast with the devastating agony of the preceding few minutes. This had felt as if someone had attacked my chest with a blunt axe and then tried to force my ribs open with bare hands. But now, apparently floating, all was at ease. There seemed to be no urgency about anything and I continued to observe the scene below me.

I could see the tops of my book-shelves and other people in the room. Stephen and the doctor continued to talk. Alison was by now holding a hand of the still motionless body. I seemed to sense that it would soon be 'time to go' and move off into the golden glow. I did not experience any idea of choice in this, and I was by no means afraid or sad to leave. Until then I had not really felt any particular sense of still having a body, but would have described the feeling as lying face down on nothing. I then became very conscious of some pull or pressure on one wrist or hand, and I could see Alison apparently holding tightly on to the equivalent hand of the body beside her. The gentle glow seemed to cloud and imperceptibly 'release' me.

I 'awoke' on the bed, Alison still holding on to my hand. The pain had returned but not with anything like the same intensity.

I cannot now recall when I was first able to tell anyone about this experience, but I have never spoken about it in any great detail. However, I did share it with Alison and she reported that her activity throughout was one of fervent prayer that I should not die. She recalled holding on to me as part of that prayerful task.

I regard this whole experience as one of the most significant, but humbling, events in my life. I believe that I have had just a glimpse of Heaven, perhaps, as it were, the outer courtyard, but I am sure that 'the best is yet to be'. I no longer have any fear of dying; I am sure that all pain ceases at death and that there is a real existence after this life. I still have to take care not to overdo things, but this limitation is usually beneficial in my activities. St. Paul puts it well when he says 'for when I am weak, then I am strong' (2 Corinthians 12: 10b).

I would like to believe that my life has been spared for some special purpose, but what I know is that Alison's fervent prayer was answered. On St. Valentine's Day 1981 she and I married each other. Stephen officiated!

In the first four verses of the 12th chapter of his second letter to the church in Corinth which ends with the phrase I've just quoted, St. Paul describes his OOBE:

> I must go on boasting. Although there is nothing to be gained, I will go on to visions and revelations from the Lord. (2) I know a man in Christ who fourteen years ago was caught up to the third heaven. Whether it was in the body or out of the body I do not know, God knows. (3) And I know that this man, whether in the body or apart from the body I do not know, but God knows, (4) was caught up to Paradise. He heard inexpressive things, things that man is not permitted to tell. (*The Holy Bible*, New International Version, Hodder & Stoughton)

Throughout this book there is a similar recurring theme; people have been reluctant to tell of their out-of-the-body experiences for all sorts of reasons. Some have thought that listeners would think that they were 'mad' or at least 'bad'. My hope is that they and others will be heartened to know that St. Paul himself did not speak of his experience very often either, preferring to be judged by the words and actions which flowed from his faith in Jesus rather than boastful accounts of his vision.

The Rt. Revd. Graham St. John-Willey,
B.Sc.(Hons.)

chapter one

WHAT IS AN OOBE?

Oh would some power the giftie gie us
To see ourselves as others see us
ROBERT BURNS

It appears that the gift has been given to us to do just that,
'To see ourselves as others see us'. Thousands of people
from all walks of life have been silently experiencing the
revelation into life and death which comes from an out-of-
the-body experience, in short an OOBE, whereby the
'spirit' leaves the physical body and can view the material
person from a different angle. This is not a dream, not a
vision, but a stark reality, which has both terrified and
exalted the people who have shared the experience. It is not
connected with drugs, alcohol or mental instability. It
affects people profoundly, as in the case of Mrs. Dickinson
of Liverpool, who states:

'I was asleep in bed when suddenly I found myself
standing at the top of the stairs. Because my daughter was
afraid of the dark, a light on the landing was left on all
night. I could see my bare feet as I descended the stairs.
When I entered the kitchen I was aware of faint moonlight
streaming through the window. I reached out for the light
switch which was immediately to my left as I entered the
room. I could see my hand touching the switch but the light
did not come on. I then realized that I could not feel the
switch and my hand somehow or other seemed to melt into
the wall behind. I was stunned with the realization that the
door behind me was still closed and that I had walked right

12

through it without opening it. This frightened me greatly. I knew I was out of my body. At once I felt myself lifted up to the ceiling and then I seemed to be hurtling through space at great speed in a sort of spiral. I then awoke back in my body.

I tried to convince myself that it was just a dream but I knew that the experience was real and quite different from any dream, and no amount of rationalizing could alter this knowledge. After that night, my whole attitude to life changed. I became aware that this life is just a part of a much wider existence. I also feel sure that it happened in order to prepare me for the events which have occurred since then. I know that with my previous attitude to life and death I would have been unable to cope with the death of my dear husband three years later.'

Our research over the past few years has resulted in an accumulation of overwhelming evidence to support the view that the physical body is but a mere shell, a material organism, the only purpose of which is simply to accommodate the real essence of the person, the spirit, and this same spirit, totally intact with the individual's consciousness and personality, has the power to release itself from the trappings of the material shell and thus allow the person to look down upon his or her physical body from a completely detached and objective viewpoint.

Many people have reported that they have been aware of other entities during out-of-the-body experiences. Sometimes it is just the feeling of a 'presence' and other times the strange unearthly companions are seen clearly or heard, as in the case of Mrs. Alcock of Spalding, Lincs., who remembers:

'I recall leaving my body asleep on the bed and floating

13

through the bedroom door and downstairs. I stood in the doorway and tried to switch on the light but found that I couldn't. My fingers seemed to come down through the switch. As I turned around I knew that there were two other 'presences' with me and although I did not know who they were, I distinctly heard one say to the other, 'We must get her back.' I felt myself being propelled by two pairs of hands, four lots of fingers, that seemed to support my back as I returned, floating up the stairs. The next thing I knew I was lying in bed back in my body.'

In many instances people recognize and hear the voices of relatives and friends who have died. A significant pattern emerges whereby the deceased relative advises the person to go back. Many people have reported a similar trend where the hands of the dead first beckon, showing that they are happy to rekindle the acquaintance, but then at a certain point in the proceedings they advise that the time is not right, and hold their hands up to stop the wanderer venturing further.

In almost all cases there is a reluctance to return to the physical world and leave the peace which is felt in this twilight dimension. What causes the return is often a sense of uncompleted work, or in the case of parents, they become aware that they are still needed to look after their children, and this compelling urge seems to be the trigger which instantly reverses the course of activitiy, resulting in re-entry to the physical body.

There seems to be some significance in hands being seen. An overwhelming number of people have reported that during their out-of-the-body experiences they have been guided by hands, sometimes belonging to loved ones who have passed on, or often to strangers. In many instances the hands are not connected to any being but are shown clearly and always seem to be visible for a definite purpose which the person understands fully, as in the case of Ted from Luton (*See 'Animals' Chapter 7*). To give examples of this we outline the following cases where hands have been seen to perform actions and to convey definite messages:

One woman who was very ill in hospital remembers first of all lying in bed in great pain after a major operation. She then floated out of her physical body and hovered above her bed, but the main thing that struck her was the fact that she was no longer in pain. She felt relieved, relaxed and quite bemused. Suddenly she felt herself floating towards the end of the hospital ward and then into what seemed to be a long, narrow, dark tunnel. At the end of the tunnel there was a dazzling light which attracted her. She felt she was travelling at great speed and she felt exhilarated and full of joy as she drew nearer and nearer to the light, which got brighter as she approached. She then became aware of hands looming out of the darkness at each side of the tunnel.

Although the hands were not connected to any bodies there were rows and rows of them, and despite the peculiar circumstances she was not in the least afraid. She had a distinct feeling that she recognized the hands, even though she could not actually see their owners. She thought she saw the hands of her long departed grandmother, whom she remembered from her childhood days and she was convinced that she saw her father's hands. He had been dead for several years. There were several pairs of hands which she did not recognize, but from which she could sense a feeling of great love. The hands and fingers seemed to beckon her forward.

Then she was overpowered with emotion when she saw a

15

pair of tiny baby hands, which seemed to come out of the darkness, appealing for her to approach. She knew in that instant that they were the hands of her dead baby. She longed to dash forward to take hold of the little fingers when she was aware of seeing her father's hands in front of her, but this time they were held with the palms towards her in a gesture which forbade her to go forward. She remembers the dilemma which she felt being halted from rushing towards her baby, but then she became aware of her other three children who were at home awaiting her return from hospital.

Again, her father's hands moved as if trying to push her back along the tunnel. In her mind she was filled with compassion for the three small children who still depended upon her so much. It appears that the moment she experienced this emotion, she had the willpower to reverse the movement, even though she felt great sadness at having to leave the dead baby, of whose presence she was acutely aware. At once she began to move backwards along the tunnel, the light at the far end becoming smaller and smaller until it resembled a pin prick. The next moment she opened her eyes, and she was back in her hospital bed, with pain surging through her.

The vivid memory of floating and moving through the tunnel, the light, the hands, the dead baby, remains fresh and real in her mind today. She knows it happened to her and it was not just a dream. She is convinced that the experience was meant to happen to her to stop her grieving for the dead baby and to apply herself to her earthly life. The main two points that are uppermost in her mind are firstly that she is no longer afraid to die, and secondly, although she always thinks about the dead child, she has a comforting feeling that the baby is being looked after by loving caring friends.

Mr Palmer's Story

Mr. Palmer of Farnborough went to bed as usual one night when he became aware of a buzzing sound that seemed to vibrate through his head. This sound was accompanied by a sinking feeling. He remembers trying to sit up in bed, but became alarmed when he found that he could not move a muscle. He thought that he had become paralysed. Again, he tried to move his arm, but no matter how much he willed himself, he could not move. However, he was able to open his eyes. The bedroom appeared perfectly normal and he could hear the night sounds from the street outside. Suddenly he had a rising feeling, as if he had floated upwards, to about thirty feet. Again he tried to move his limbs but this seemed to make him spin round and round, so he stopped trying to move and remained floating.

At this time he was living in a bed-sit in a large old Victorian house. It entered his head that if he wanted to, he would be able to float anywhere in the house, so it occurred to him that he could travel to the floor above where a certain girl had a room in the house. He remembered working it all out in his mind, and he was aware of having read somewhere that the only thing necessary to be able to travel off to any particular place was to think about that place and it would happen. He thought about the girl's bedroom, and in that split second he found himself standing in the middle of her room. He wanted to turn round towards her bed to look at the sleeping girl but, as he turned, two large hands, not attached to anything, appeared in front of his eyes, preventing him from seeing the girl. He remembers getting the clear message in his head: *'This experience is not meant for spying on people'*. The next thing he knew he was floating back down towards his body.

Mrs. Brown's Story

Mrs. Brown relates the story of how she awoke one night to find her room filled with what she could only describe as swirling mist. She thought this most odd and at once looked across to the window to see if it had been left open. She saw that it was closed, but the curtains were still giving the impression of a breeze coming into the room. She then heard the most wonderful music unlike anything she had ever heard before. She thought at once that one of her sons must have left the radio on in the downstairs room. She raised herself up in the bed to get up and go downstairs to switch off the music when suddenly there before her, hovering in mid-air, she saw the most beautiful pair of hands.

'I was not frightened at all, even though it was a strange thing to see. The hands were absolutely perfect, like those of a ballerina. One of the hands reached forward as if to take my hand to help me up out of bed. Just as I was about to grasp the hand I turned my head back for some reason, and then I became petrified when I saw my sleeping body lying behind me on the bed. At that moment I looked back round. The hands had vanished and I felt myself sliding back down into my physical body. The following morning I awoke and the first thing I did was to go over to check the windows to make sure that they had been properly closed the night before. They were locked. I will never forget the experience. It was short and simple but it has changed my whole outlook on life, because I know I was not dreaming and I really did see the hands and I heard that music.'

chapter two

THE LIGHT

Mrs Ellis' Story

At 3.00 a.m. David Ellis answered the telephone. 'It's your wife,' said the nurse. 'She's had a relapse. She's failing fast. The doctor wonders if you would like to come into the hospital straight away.'

Mr. Ellis answered in a panic, 'But what about the children?'

'Can't you get a neighbour to keep an eye on them?'

'Yes. Yes. I'll see what I can do. How is she? Is she critical?'

'I think you'd better come in.'

Mr. Ellis telephoned his sister who lived nearby and told her that he'd leave the key outside the back door, under the mat. He got to the hospital, shaking with fright, and rushed to his wife's bedside.

'She's lost a lot of blood,' explained the nurse.

'She'll be OK though. I mean she won't...'

'We're doing everything we can. Would you like a cup of tea?'

'Can I talk to the doctor?'

The nurse nodded sympathetically and left the room.

As he took hold of his wife's hand she opened her eyes and looked up at him. He was sure that she recognized him, although she didn't say anything. It hurt him to see her eyes so full of pain. Slowly they closed and she became still. The room was silent. He glanced over at the heart monitor in horror.

'No! No! Marjorie, come back!' The monitor displayed a long, continuous, straight line.

As Mr. Ellis sobbed over his dead wife, little did he know that he was being watched. As Marjorie had closed her eyes, she had experienced the bewildering feeling of slipping out of her physical body, with all her senses intact.

'One minute I was tortured in pain,' she recalls, 'The next I seemed to be floating upwards until I reached the ceiling, where I remained, hovering. The main thing I kept thinking was, 'I've got no pain now – what a great relief.' After a few seconds I seemed to get used to this floating sensation, then I began to become aware of what had happened. Down below me I could see my body lying on the bed, and I remember feeling horribly confused because I could see my husband crying over me. 'What's wrong with him?' I thought. 'Can't he see me? Doesn't he know I'm all right now?'

Then Marjorie's attention was drawn to the heart monitoring machine by the bedside. She watched the long steady green line. 'It was only when I noticed the line on the machine that I realised what was going on. Just beforehand the machine had been showing a zig-zag pattern. Then it dawned on me that I must be dead, although I could hardly believe it, I felt so well and peaceful.'

Just then the nurse returned with the cup of tea. 'I saw the alarmed look on her face as she rang the emergency bell. Within seconds the room was filled with people all rushing around. First they gave me mouth-to-mouth resuscitation, then a nurse injected a large needle into my chest. I could see clearly what the nurse was doing, and I was bewildered at the fact that I could not feel the pain of the needle. Then they gave me a heart massage, then electric shock treatment. I was amazed as I watched my physical body writhe on the bed then fall back into its state of stillness. Gradually the medical staff left the room. I watched the doctor put his hand on my husband's shoulder and then shake his head.

'I'm all right though', I kept calling to my husband. 'See! I'm up here, I'm fine.' I remember becoming quite upset when he just ignored me. Again I called out desperately trying to make him hear me. He simply bent over, kissed my still white face and walked out of the room.

'I kept wondering why he hadn't answered me. I was shouting as loud as I could.

'Then a nurse and hospital porter entered the room. They lifted my body onto a trolley and placed a sheet over me. I followed the porter as he wheeled the trolley down a long corridor. I floated behind the porter into the hospital mortuary. A wave of shock hit me as I realised what was happening. As I watched my body on the trolley the scene suddenly misted over. The mortuary faded and I felt myself floating along a marble-like passage. At the end of the passage was an extremely bright light – brighter than anything I had ever seen before. I felt myself strongly attracted towards the light and was, at the same time, engulfed in a feeling of warmth and comfort. Then, as if from the midst of this light, there appeared lots of hands stretching out towards me.

'I felt so happy and carefree and I had an overwhelming feeling of being loved. The strange thing was that although there were no bodies or faces connected with the hands, I seemed to know instinctively who they all belonged to. There was my nan, my dad and several other relations and friends, all of whom had been long dead. It was then I noticed them – a pair of tiny perfect hands were beckoning to me. I knew deep in my heart that they were the little hands of my dead baby. I longed to rush over and grasp them. They seemed to be saying, "I love you, I love you" over and over again. I've never felt so loved before or since. I reached out to them as they came nearer and nearer to me.

'I then heard the firm voice of my father telling me, "You can't come yet, you've a lot to do. Your children need you, especially Julie." (Julie is my youngest child.)

'Despite my father's words, I still wanted so much to go forward to the dead baby, even though I was fully aware at the time that I loved all my other children and my husband as well. I struggled with myself for ages, and it seemed to me that I had no strength to turn back. It was then that I heard my nan's voice ringing out in support of my father. She too was trying to persuade me to go back. In an instant I felt a wave of pity for my other children who were depending on me, and my heart went out to my husband, as I remembered his grief-stricken face. In that split-second, like a thunder-bolt, I was hurled back into my physical body.

'The first thing that occurred to me was that something was irritating my face – something seemed to be covering it. As I raised my hand to pull away the covering, a piercing scream made me open my eyes. I just caught sight of a young nurse as she fainted down onto the mortuary floor.

'A minute or so later the nurse was peering down at me. I'll never forget the terrified expression on her face. I reached out my hand towards her. I only wanted to comfort her, but she ran screaming from the room.

'After that, the mortuary was filled with doctors and nurses. One young blonde nurse with a sweet face bent over and whispered, "So you've decided to come back!"

Marjorie made a rapid recovery. Soon she was out of hospital back home with her adoring husband and children.

'I shall never forget the love and peace I felt – even now it makes me feel warm all over. I think I became a better person – less selfish, kinder and certainly happier and more contented with this life. I have the inner conviction that there is no need to panic about things now. I just take life as it comes. My dad was right when he told me that my family needed me, especially Julie.'

Jean Wilson's Story
As they left the cinema young Jean Wilson and her best friend Kate made their way towards the local hamburger bar to have a quick bite to eat before they went home.

'What's the matter with you tonight?' asked Jean, noticing that her friend was unusually quiet.

'Oh nothing. It doesn't matter.'

'Come on – what's troubling you?'

'Well,' replied Kate hesitantly, 'Remember that new clerk I told you about?'

'Oh don't tell me you're bothered about him,' quipped Jean. 'Remember what my dad told us – "Men are like buses – Never run after them, another one will be along in a minute." Jean stopped talking when she saw that her friend was not laughing. In a more serious tone she urged Kate to share her problem.

'It's just that he took me out the other night, like I told you.' After a pause, Kate continued: 'Well, I found out today that he's invited Debbie to his friend's birthday party tomorrow night.'

'So?'

'There! I knew you wouldn't understand. Let's just forget it.'

They munched their burgers without further conversation until Jean suggested, 'Why don't we have our own party tomorrow night? We could invite a few people round to our place. I'm sure my mum wouldn't mind.'

Kate looked unimpressed. 'You still don't realise, do you?'

'What's wrong now? I'm only trying to help.'

'It's no use,' answered Kate. 'If I can't go out with Tony, I don't want to go out with anyone at all.'

Kate put down her knife and fork and got up to leave the table. She thanked Jean for trying to help, then added, 'But it's useless.'

Next evening, Jean was at home with her parents. 'I was standing in the kitchen and suddenly began to feel quite ill. First I got very cold and the next moment I felt as if I was burning up, feeling sick and faint. I tried to make my way to the front room to tell my parents that I wasn't feeling well when everything went black and I remember falling to the floor just inside the back door.

'I was quite surprised to hear Kate's voice, and I remember thinking to myself that she must have decided to call round to our house after all. I hoped she wouldn't be too disappointed to find that there was no party. My next recollection was of walking with Kate towards what I can only describe as a vast calm black sea. I then realised that far out across the sea there was an extremely bright light. It became brighter and more dazzling by the second. At first we just stood at the edge of the water and stared at the light. I was overcome by its power.

'I watched Kate slowly wade into the water. She turned back to me and waved for me to follow her. I was beginning to feel afraid. I didn't move. She called out to me to follow her. She kept calling me over and over again. "Come with

25

me. Come with me." For some reason I felt paralysed. My feet would not move. It was as if I was cemented down on to the earth. As I watched Kate wade deeper and deeper into the water I began to feel even more apprehensive, but at the same time there was something about the light that had a strange calming effect. It's just that I seemed to be caught between two directions. I could see Kate moving further away from me and still I could hear her voice crying after me to go with her.

'In a flash, my mind started sending me messages not to follow her, even if I could have moved my feet, although at the same time I seemed to know that if I did choose to follow her no real harm would have come to me. It was a most peculiar feeling. I remember shouting out, "I must go back. I can't come with you. No."

'The next thing I knew, I was wakening up on the couch in the front room, with my worried-looking parents tending to me. I told them nothing of what I had just experienced. The doctor was duly called in and it turned out that I was suffering from food poisoning. The doctor left a prescription for me, advising that I should go straight to bed.

'I dozed off to sleep, but on awakening later that night I was concerned to see my mother's saddened face.

'"What's the matter? What did the doctor tell you? Why are you looking so worried?," I asked.

'"I've just had a phone call from Kate's father," replied my mother grimly. "Kate committed suicide this evening."

Barbara Horrsbury's Story
When Mrs. Barbara Horrsbury was admitted to hospital suffering from a massive haemorrhage, she was placed in a bed and the curtains were pulled around so that she could

not see anything else that was going on in the small ward. Suddenly, she slipped out of her body and hovered in mid-air from where she saw another patient being wheeled into a bed opposite hers. She watched from just underneath the ceiling, and peering down, Barbara could see that the patient who had just been brought in was wearing a pink nightgown. She watched a nurse place a vase of daffodils on the patient's locker.

She then found herself in a long dark tunnel which had a bright light at the end of it. The next moment she felt herself being swooshed back along the tunnel and into her body again. Shortly after, the nurse pulled back the curtains which were surrounding her bed and there, sure enough, across the room was the other patient in the pink nightgown, with the vase of daffodils on her locker.

Mrs. Neale's Story

Mrs. Edith Neale also had the feeling of slipping out of her physical body, then travelling down a very long tunnel towards a brilliant light which seemed to illuminate the entire end section of the tunnel.

'I heard the most heavenly music and was filled with great joy and peace. I became aware of someone travelling beside me. I looked across and saw my niece, June. June had been in an accident and was in hospital at the same time, recovering from serious injuries. She smiled and waved to me saying, "Come on in, Auntie Edie, don't be afraid." I heard myself answer, "Not yet, love, I've got a lot of work to do, but I'll be seeing you soon."

'Everything went black after that and I don't remember anything more except being aware that I was safely back in my own bed.

'The next day I was at work as usual when I got a phone call from my distraught sister to tell me that June had suffered a relapse and had died in the middle of the night.

'I never told my sister or anyone else about the tunnel or the light, but on the day of June's funeral, June's brother put his hand on my arm and asked me if I had been in the hospital corridor on the night June had died.

'I told him, no of course I hadn't been there or I would have gone straight into the ward.

'"That's what I thought," answered my nephew, "It's just that before she died June kept saying, 'There's Auntie Edie out there – she can see me.'"

chapter three

VANTAGE VIEWPOINT

Frances and David's Story

Frances was on holiday in the south of France with her boyfriend Dave. They had gone down to the beach on Dave's motorbike. Frances went into the sea for a swim, leaving Dave on the beach. She was an excellent swimmer and was splashing about in the warm sunshine having a lovely time when, suddenly, she got caught up in a freak wave formation.

'I did not fully realize what was happening and certainly I cannot recall feeling in any real danger of drowning. There was a split-second awareness that something was wrong. The next instant I found, to my amazement, that I was hovering in the air about three or four feet above the waves. Incredible as it may sound, I was suspended in mid air. I looked all around me, then I remember looking back towards the beach where people were just lying on the sand, some under big umbrellas.

'Everything seemed so normal, apart from me, that is. Something immediately below me caught my eye. I realized it was an arm sticking up out of the water. The arm was waving around and then it disappeared below the waves. I kept watching and I saw first the fingers appear back out of the water, then the hand and eventually the whole arm. It was only then, as I watched the arm go under the water again, that I realized the arm belonged to me! The horrible, frightening truth dawned on me. I was watching myself drown!

'I tried to call out to people on the beach. I opened my

mouth but no sound came out. Somehow, I managed to lower myself down towards the spot where I had seen my arm go under the water. I was aware of trying to stretch out my arm but my fingers seemed to melt through the water.

'I couldn't feel any sensation of touching the turbulent water. The more I tried to feel underneath the waves to try and grasp hold of my physical arm, the more it felt like I was just waving my hand through thin air.

'When once more I tried to shout for help I noticed that three young men were running into the water towards me. "At last," I thought, "I've been heard." I could see my boyfriend and some other people standing on the beach looking out to sea. As the young men got nearer to me I started to wave to them. I could see by their special clothes that they were life guards. I called out to them but I felt disappointed that all three of them totally ignored me.

'I watched the life guards fish my body out of the sea and I followed them back on to the beach where they stretched my body down on the sand. One man started to give me the kiss-of-life. I watched as they went through various procedures to try to revive my body which remained deathly still.

'It was at this point that I noticed my boyfriend standing nearby. He was watching the life guards with a ghastly white face. He seemed to be in a state of absolute shock. I heard the life guards tell him that they were not able to bring me round, then I watched him dash away and get on his motorbike. I decided to follow him to see what he was up to.

'I watched Dave start up the engine and take off at speed. He drove very fast, but I remember thinking how easy it was to keep up with him, just by moving through the air above the bike. It was just like flying, only without an aeroplane. I kept going at the same speed as the machine. It was quite an exhilarating feeling, much better than sitting on the pillion. As Dave increased his speed I felt myself speed up automatically. At one point I called to him to look up, but he didn't take any notice of me.

'We came to a sharp bend on the road and I screamed out in horror as the wheels of the motorbike skidded and I watched Dave smash down on to the road. The motorbike slid along for a few yards, then came to a halt by the side banking. I could only stare at Dave, sprawled down on the ground. I was very relieved to see him move, so I knew he was still conscious.

'I hovered around Dave for a while, feeling completely helpless. I kept talking to him, trying to comfort him, but he took no notice of me whatsoever. Then I began to wonder what was happening to my own body back on the beach. No sooner had the thought entered my head than I felt myself speeding back along the road, through the air, towards the beach.'

'When I arrived, I saw one of the life guards pump down on my chest. I noticed that one of the other life guards was kneeling beside my body. The man was crying. I got the impression that he thought I was dead, yet I felt perfectly fine and healthy, with no aches or pains whatsoever. I felt sorry for this man, so I moved up beside him and touched his arm as if to say that I was all right and he needn't worry. I got such a shock though when my hand went right through his skin. I just could not stop my fingers from passing right through his arm.

'I felt puzzled at this stage, and became frustrated at not being able to make my presence felt. I looked down at my washed out body lying lifeless in the sand. The lifeguards had stopped working on me by this time. They were just watching for a few moments, then I heard them start to talk between themselves in lowered tones. I could speak fluent French, so I could understand what they were saying. They all agreed that I was dead and there was nothing they could do for me. They arranged that one of them would stay with my body whilst the others went to their base to inform the police and to report my death to their supervisor.

'Suddenly I was faced with a distinct choice. I knew at that point that it was my last chance to decide whether to stay as I was or whether I should go back to my body. I knew deep down inside me that I did not want to die and as if in a flash I found myself back in my body. I could feel the sand sticking to my back as I felt my weight press down on the ground.

'I opened my eyes and I heard one of the lifeguards cry out to the others telling them that I was back. They came running over towards me, all of them quite excited. They fussed around me for a few minutes and seemed surprised that I was able to pick myself up off the ground and walk away.

'I picked up my belongings from the beach and made my way back to the hotel where I was staying with Dave. I quietly opened the door of our room and entered. I could see Dave standing across the far side of the room beside a mirror. Our eyes met in the mirror, he spun round with a stunned expression and just stared at me in silence.

'It's all right, you can relax, I'm not a ghost,' I reassured him. I walked over to him and kissed his face, which was grazed and bruised. I told him that he really ought to be more careful of that motorbike of his. I told him that I had

32

seen him take that bend like a madman. He stared hard at me and asked me what I was talking about. How could I have seen him? All I could answer was, 'It's a long story.'

Paul Picken's Story
Paul Picken used to work as a bath attendant at a coalmine in the English Midlands. One Saturday night when he was on night duty on his own, he began to feel very sleepy. He made himself a cup of tea to see if that would keep him awake, but still he could hardly keep his eyes open.

'About 2.00 a.m. I lay down on top of a long bunker and started to read a book, but eventually I dozed off to sleep. I felt myself rise up out of my body and on looking down I could see my body stretched out peacefully on the bunker, still holding the book which had fallen onto my chest.

'I felt perfectly natural floating around the room and I remember although I was puzzled at being in two places at once, I had no fear whatsoever. It was if I was in my true state of being as I floated around the room. I was totally aware of what was going on at all times, and thought it interesting that the 'me' floating around was the part that housed all my awareness and consciousness. When I looked down on my body sprawled out on the bunker, I couldn't help feeling how insignificant my physical shell really was. It didn't appear to have any mind of its own, all the thinking power was up in the air with me.

'Within a very short period, I started to feel myself drawn out of the room. I was compelled to follow the instinct which led me towards a ladder. I used this regularly to get up on the roof of the baths. I floated towards it, but when I put my hand out to grasp hold of the sides of the ladder, my hand just went right through the metal and try as I would, I just could not get a grip on the thing. It was then that I realized how silly I'd been and I thought to myself that if I can float upwards, who needs a ladder? The minute that thought came into my head, up I went right on to the roof of the baths.

'Now, unbeknown to anyone else at the colliery, because I was responsible for the safety of all the goods in the baths, I had previously drilled a tiny hole in the roof, so that I could look through this from up above to keep an eye on the locker area directly below without anyone knowing that I was checking.

'For some reason I felt myself drawn towards the section of the roof where this small hole was. I found that I could see down through the floor into the locker area. I was quite surprised to see two men going along the line of lockers and searching all through their fellow workers' belongings. They had either a key or some small gadget which they were sharing to open the doors of the lockers. I recognized both men instantly and I must say that I was surprised. I would never have guessed that they would have done such a thing in a million years.

'I floated back down the ladder, then looked through a window into the room where I could see my body still stretched out on top of the bunker, fast asleep. I approached my body with some trepidation, not quite knowing what to do to get back into myself.

'I stood beside my sleeping body for a while, wondering what I should do. The only thing I could think of was to lie down in the same position on top of the bunker. It must have done the trick although I don't remember anything very clearly about how I managed to merge back into my physical body. I looked at the clock and it was 2.10 a.m. I had only been asleep for about ten minutes. The one overpowering thought in my mind was of the two men I had caught robbing the lockers.

'I immediately made my way to the locker area of the baths and sure enough, there I saw the rows of lockers with some of the doors visibly ajar, where they had been forced open.

'The next morning I felt compelled to go to my boss and report exactly what had happened, although I admit it did take me some courage to find the right words to describe how I managed to catch the thieves red-handed.

'I think my boss thought I was raving mad to start with. I had a feeling though that he began to believe me just a little bit when I freely admitted having allowed myself to fall asleep. You see, that was strictly against all the rules, and both the boss and I knew it. He could see that I was so certain of my facts that I was willing to put my own job on the line.

'The outcome of the story was that the police were called in to investigate the thefts and the two men in question were discovered to have the stolen goods in their keeping. A court hearing was arranged, the men were charged and dismissed from their employment.'

Bill Crocker's Story
It started when Bill heard a loud buzzing sound in his head, then the next thing he knew he was floating in the air in his bedroom. 'I looked down and could see myself and my wife lying in bed. I quickly became accustomed to my new condition and began to feel quite bemused at the sudden realization that I could fly. I was aware of passing straight through my bedroom window and out into the night air. I

was able to direct myself so that if I had the desire to turn any particular way or if I wanted to go slower or faster, higher or lower, all I had to do was wish this, and it would happen.

'I directed myself towards a particular area of town but I was surprised to find that the normal modern office block was not there. Instead, in the exact same place, there stood a somewhat shabby tenement building, totally unknown to me. I floated through a door and found myself in a dim corridor which led to a stairway. I floated up the stairway and I remember getting the distinct feeling that I was not in the present time. There was something about the structure of the staircase, the landings and the door designs that gave me the feeling that I was somewhere in the past, although I noticed that there were electric lights on at the time, therefore it cannot have been too far back in the past.

'All at once I met a small boy who came wandering along one of the landings towards me, stopping by the top of the staircase. The child was about five years of age and was quite talkative. I exchanged a few words with the boy and we seemed to be getting on fine. The child wore short trousers and little laced boots.

'There didn't seem anything especially out of the ordinary about him. He struck me as a likeable little chap, with a dirty face and a freckled nose.

'Suddenly one of the landing doors opened and a young woman came out. She took one look at me and started to scream blue murder. At that stage I began to feel alarmed. I could see the terror on her face and that started me off. I felt terrified although I wasn't sure why. I stood there, staring hard at her, then she dashed over towards me, grabbed the little boy off his feet, ran back in through the doorway and

36

slammed the door behind her. The next thing I knew, I was back in bed beside my wife.

'I am convinced that I had a time slip of some description. There was something about the woman's hairstyle and the floral wrap-around apron that suggested the 1940s to me, although I can't be sure.

'I'll never forget the look on that woman's face. I know I'm not the best-looking chap in the world, but she was overdoing it a bit. The funny thing was, though, the child didn't seem to be one bit bothered by my presence. He just gabbed away to me like I was his dad or his uncle, but the woman definitely acted as if she's seen a ghost. When I think about it now, I sometimes wonder if she was right. Maybe she did see me as that. Maybe to her I was a ghost.

'The following day, just out of interest, I walked down to that part of town. The towering office block stood dominating the scene. There were no tenement buildings and no women in wrap-around aprons.'

Derek Scott's Story
It was a sunny afternoon. Derek Scott was travelling down the motorway towards his home in Cardiff when the nightmare happened. Before he knew what was happening, his car was ploughing into a heap of piled up vehicles spread right across the motorway. Derek was taken to the nearest hospital in bad shape, with broken bones, cuts and bruises.

'The doctor gave me some sort of jab, and to tell you the truth, I might have put my experience down to that, if I hadn't seen the proof for myself.

'I was just lying in the bed with the doctor and nurse attending to me. I was in terrible pain and felt like crying

37

out. The next second I found myself hovering up near the ceiling. I just couldn't believe it. Two main things struck me. The first thing was that the pain had vanished and I·was feeling really relaxed and light-hearted with not a care in the world. The other thing was that I could see myself lying below on the bed quite clearly. I could see everything, the nurse was fussing around the bed and the doctor was sitting down reading something, I'm not sure what. I looked just like a corpse but I wasn't really bothered. I think I was more tickled than anything.

'After a short time, I got used to the feeling of weightless-ness and then I found to my amusement that I could, somehow or other, navigate myself around the room, a small side ward with only my bed in it.

'I could go close up against the ceiling and I got the feeling that I could have gone straight up through it if I had wanted to, but I was more curious about what was happening to my physical body, and I suppose that kept me in the room.

'I noticed that the lighting system was attached not to the ceiling, but to one of the walls. There was a long strip light running almost the entire length of the wall behind the bed. From my bird's eye viewpoint I could see that the light was attached to the wall by a metal structure.

'Above the light, running almost the same length along the wall, I noticed that there was a narrow wooden shelf. Something caught my attention. From just below the ceiling I could look right down behind the light-strip and I could distinctly see that a card had got caught deep down in the space between the light and the wall. For some reason I kept staring at that card. I couldn't make out the picture because of the way it was lying.

'There was a kind of swoosh and then I found myself back in the bed with the pain seering through my body once more. The first words I uttered were, 'Nurse, there's a card up there behind that light.' The nurse just smiled patiently and took absolutely no notice of my words. It was only after I repeated myself again and again that she started to take notice. She argued that there was nothing up there and I was just suffering from shock. I insisted that I knew there was a card trapped behind the light. I was told to settle down, then the nurse added that there was no way I could have seen behind that light.

'Even though I was in agony, I was determined to make the nurse listen to me, and again stressed that I did see down behind the light and that I saw a card trapped down there. I told her that I had been hovering up in the air. At that point I nearly lost heart when I saw the look of disbelief on the nurse's face, but I was so sure that I had seen the card I made myself ask her to have a look behind the light fixture.

'Giving me an odd look, and without saying a word, the nurse impatiently pulled a chair across to the wall, stood up on it and tried to see behind the light. I told her to look over to her right a bit. She felt behind the metal attachment and then looked down at me with a stunned expression as she fished out an old yellowed get-well card from behind the light.'

chapter four

PARADISE?

The Simpson Family's Story
The Simpson family were preparing for Christmas. Mum
had confided in the eldest boy that, for the benefit of the two
younger children who still believed in Santa Claus, Dad was
going to dress up as Father Christmas to give them a
surprise. There were only two weeks to go and there was a
lot to do.

That night Mr Simpson went to visit a friend who was a
scout master. The man had promised to lend him a Father
Christmas outfit, a relic of the previous year's scout
concert. The children were fast asleep in bed when Mrs
Simpson answered a ring on her doorbell. She was taken
aback to find two policemen standing outside. She invited
them in out of the snow.

After the policemen left, Mrs Simpson sat on the end of
her bed. 'It felt as if my whole world had fallen apart. How
was I going to tell the children there would be no Santa
Claus that year. How was I going to tell them their father
had just been killed?

'In a state of shock I walked around the house looking at
all of the rooms, each filled with memories of my husband. I
checked and re-checked the children as they all slept
peacefully. I gazed down at their calm, slumbering little
faces, dreading the next morning when they would wake up
and have to face life without their Dad.

'I walked downstairs to the kitchen to make myself a cup
of tea. The first thing I saw as I entered the room was the
cluster of fairy-lights on the kitchen table. My husband had

been checking the bulbs to make sure they were safe. I remembered the last words he ever spoke to me: "Remember love, don't touch these till I get back, I don't want anything to happen to you."

'I collapsed down on the kitchen chair, tears streaming down my cheeks. I think I was at my lowest ebb at that moment. I felt so bad I didn't know how I would find the strength to carry on living. It was as if nothing mattered anymore. I just sat there for ages, gazing at the walls, then my eye was attracted by some bright red crepe paper. I think that seemed to jolt me back to reality. I had just bought some rolls of brightly coloured paper that afternoon to give to my little girl for her school party. She was going to help the teacher make some fancy hats.

'The thought of the children's party and those coloured hats made me realize that life somehow had to go on. The more I thought about it, the more I knew that all my attention and energy was going to be needed to help the children through the terrible days and weeks that lay ahead.

'I walked back upstairs and got into bed. I didn't even bother to take off my dressing gown. I lay in bed, staring into the darkness until I sobbed myself to sleep. A while later, something made me stir in my sleep. I woke up and got out of bed. I wrapped my dressing gown around myself and walked towards the bottom of the bed.

'I was stopped in my tracks when I saw a little box a short way in front of me. It seemed to be hovering in mid air, surrounded by a strange light. I turned round to see if the bedside lamp was on and I got the fright of my life when I saw myself lying asleep on the bed. I looked down at myself from where I was standing. I felt perfectly real. I even remember pinching myself. That felt real too. I could not

41

understand why there were two of me. I kept watching the other me in the bed. I was so confused.

'I turned back round and I could still see the little box in front of me, with the mysterious light surrounding it. I recognized it this time. It was a little wooden trinket box which had belonged to my husband's mother. That brought everything back to my mind with crashing reality.

'I looked back at my body lying in the big bed and I thought that I must have died in my sleep. I started to float upwards. I couldn't stop myself and when I could not control this drifting, I got really frightened. I could feel my heart beating faster and faster and I got more and more terrified.

'I floated right up to the ceiling. I just seemed to pass right through the plaster and then up through the loft and right up to the roof and outside.

'I became aware of an extremely bright light somewhere above me. I looked towards it and there, standing in a long, white robe, stood my husband. He looked so much younger. He just stood there smiling at me with a happy, relaxed expression on his face. He seemed quite serene and radiant. He stretched out his hand to me. I ran to him and he led me by the hand to the most beautiful place I have ever seen in my life.

'We entered a room which was filled with a warm light. I tried to work our where this light was coming from as there didn't appear to be any shadows. It was nothing like our ordinary sunlight, that seems dull in comparison.

'In the room there were the most exquisite flower arrangements. The shapes and colours of these flowers were beyond anything I had seen before. I doubt if I could have imagined such creations and some were of colours I'd never seen before.

'Suddenly into this room came my husband's parents, who were both dead. They greeted me warmly and spoke to me. When I remarked about the beautiful flowers, my husband told me, "Mum grows them. She has plenty of time now." He then took me over to one side and explained to me, "You remember how Mum always loved to potter about in the garden? This is her latest work." He pointed to some lilies which were just too incredible to explain in ordinary words.

'My husband explained to me that his parents had just come to see me again. They embraced me and both of them left. My husband then told me that I was standing in our own house, the house he was preparing for me. Something outside moved, and made me walk towards the doorway. There outside in the most charming garden was Charlie, our faithful gardener, who had passed away the previous year. I asked my husband what Charlie was doing here. He told me that Charlie was keeping the garden in shape, of course, and then added that the old man's bad knee was all better now.

'My husband told me that Charlie was helping him to get everything ready for when I was to join them, but he assured me that there was no rush. He explained to me that he was praying for me and the children and that they needed me very much. That was why I couldn't stay with him in our new house.

'I felt so comforted by his words, and I knew from then on that there was no need to grieve any more because I could see that he was very much alive and waiting for me.

'The next instant I found myself waking up in my own bed. I felt a deep calm inside, and although I missed his constant presence desperately I knew that one day we would be together again.

'I never told the children about my strange encounter with their father, although on many occasions I was tempted to. Especially that Christmas, when they were crying for their Dad, I longed to tell them, but I felt they were all too young. Their little minds wouldn't have been able to take it. The only thing that pulled me through those bleak days was the knowledge that he was looking after us. That gave me the strength to give the children the help and guidance they needed.'

chapter five

THE HEALING FORCE

The positive force which is utilized in healing seems to be available for anyone who cares to call upon it. Very often the people who work with this force do not attribute any particular personal gifts to the healing power, as in the case of Matthew Manning, who is reputed to be Britain's leading healer. He feels the force is God given, but can be used by almost anyone and he certainly has no illusions about his own role: 'I don't know why God chose me. He must have been joking.'

Sister May's Story

In an old run-down church hall in Northampton, a location that looks more like a closed-down cinema than a place of miracles, there gathers together a cross-section of Christian clergymen, including representatives of the Anglican, Baptist and Reform Churches, Methodists, Roman Catholics, Congregationalists and other religions. They meet on the third Thursday in each month and in the name of Jesus they lay hands upon the sick and bring about true healing.

One of the healers who occasionally attends these meetings when visiting the town is a charismatic lady called Sister May (The Rt. Revd. E. May Richards D.D.) who hails from the United States and who, before her conversion, used to make her living by running a brothel! One night a voice echoed round her room telling her she had to change her life. She was an alcoholic at the time, but from that moment she never touched a drop of alcohol, and has spent the last forty years of her life travelling all around the world, healing people. She announces to everyone that the healing has nothing to do with her personally. She is convinced that she is a channel through which the grace of God flows. By placing her hands upon the afflicted, she transmits the healing energy onwards towards the patient.

One day in a small Mexican village, Sister May opened her door to find a very small crippled boy all alone on her doorstep. 'There was no sign of anyone else anywhere, so I brought the child in thinking he was lost and that his parents would surely arrive any minute. He was only about four years of age, and was severely crippled and could not walk at all. He was terrified and shook so much that the first thing I did was to very gently speak to him, taking his hands and telling him that everything would be just fine. As the hours went by there was still no sign of any parents, and the boy had no idea of his address and, in fact, hardly spoke a word.

'Not knowing quite what to do, I got down on my knees and started to pray for guidance. It suddenly became clear to me that the child had been sent to me for a reason. I looked at his little twisted legs and at once I was overcome with compassion. I held out my hand for the boy to join me in prayer. I said the words out loud and waited for him to repeat them. Very slowly and shyly the child responded. This was the breakthrough.

'I made him a meal and then waited and waited, but still there was no sign of anyone. It became apparent that I would have to deal with the sitaution as best I could.

'For three days the child stayed with me. I worked out a little routine, whereby every morning after breakfast we would pray together and simply ask Jesus to straighten out the child's legs. I laid my hands on the frail limbs and very gradually I could see the knotted muscles relax and the legs start to straighten out. The more this happened, the more excited the child became and, of course, the more he co-operated.

'Each afternoon the praying continued and on the morning of the third day, I held the little boy steady and watched him take two or three tottering steps. More praying followed, and by late afternoon the child had completely regained his confidence, and was able to walk about the house without any assistance from me at all. That evening there was a knock at my door. I opened it to find a timid looking woman on the doorstep.

'The woman told me that she had left her crippled child on my doorstep three days ago. She asked me if he was still with me. I told the woman that I was sorry, but I had no crippled child with me.

'At that moment the little boy came running from the house calling for his mother. The woman almost collapsed in tears as she hugged her child, thanking me over and over again. I explained that it had nothing to do with me, and I asked her to remember to thank Jesus.'

Anne's Story
Anne had been suffering from severe abdominal pains. She went to her doctor, who referred her to a specialist who eventually informed her that she had diverticulitis – an incurable condition of the bowel. 'As the weeks went past I found that I was in constant pain, and was growing weaker and weaker in body and spirit. I returned time and time again to my doctor for stronger medication, but still the pain persisted and only got worse. Things got to breaking point as Christmas was approaching and one of my sons

announced that he was bringing his American girlfriend home to spend the holidays with the family.

'I was a complete wreck. I could hardly drag myself out of bed to do the shopping and go about the house. With my mother to look after, who is blind, the thought of having a guest over the Christmas period was almost too much for me. I just didn't know how I was going to cope with all the preparations, yet, for my son's sake, I knew I had to somehow make the effort.

'My doctor told me that he could not prescribe anything stronger for the pain and that I would just have to learn to live with it.

'A Christian friend told me that in times of tribulation she always read Psalm 16 in the Good News Bible entitled "A Prayer of Confidence". I was never particularly religious, although I believed in God in a general sort of way. Anyway, I began to read this Psalm every day. Then one day my Bible opened at James 5, 13-15. I just knew that I wanted to go for Christian healing. Up to then I went to church sometimes because I just thought it was my duty to do so. I found out that about ten miles away there were Christian healing services at Trinity Methodist Church in Northampton.

'On December 6th I arrived at the church with my husband. I felt somewhat apprehensive because I was unsure about what was going to happen. Lots of smiling faces greeted us, and set us at ease straight away. During the service there were prayers composed by members of the Order of St. Luke, who is the patron saint of physicians. Then it was announced that anyone who wished for healing should come forward to either sit or kneel and to pray with any one of the ministers, asking for healing in the name of Jesus.

'I went forward to kneel in front of a minister. I was so weak and wobbly on my feet that I could only make it as far as the first man in the line, who happened to be a black Pentecostal minister. He started to pray over me and put his hands on my head. The rest of the congregation were singing hymns. By this time I was very calm and I did not feel nervous at all. The minister suggested I pray along with him in my own words for the particular healing I wanted. I asked Jesus to make me whole in body, mind and spirit. That was all I could think of to say at the time. Then the minister annointed me with oil, and I returned to my seat. I felt an inner peace and I was happy that I had made the effort to come to this service.

'The next morning I was awakened by the dog barking. I was worried that someone was trying to break into the house and I was afraid that my mother would be alarmed.

'My husband had left for work earlier, so I had to investigate myself. I couldn't see anyone near the house so I went back inside and made myself a cup of tea, then started to prepare my mother's breakfast.

'It was only when my mother asked me how I was that I realized that I had not taken my usual morning medication, which was crucial to stave off the pain before I could attempt to eat or drink anything. It was then it hit me like a thunderbolt – *FOR THE FIRST TIME IN ALMOST A YEAR I WAS COMPLETELY FREE FROM PAIN*.

'That was four years ago, and I have not even had the slightest twinge of pain since. My complaint had completely vanished. My doctor is baffled and just cannot offer any explanation. The effect of the healing was so great upon the entire family that my husband, who had patiently shared the misery of my illness, has since become a minister in a church.'

Fred's Story

During the First World War a group of refugees took shelter in a small vilage situated on a high plateau in the Ardennes, just south-east of Liege in Belgium. They sought the protection of the Virgin Mary, and consecrated the village to her, changing its name from Banneux to Banneux Notre Dame. Although the other surrounding villages were destroyed and burnt to the ground, Banneux was spared and to this day stands as a shrine to Our Lady.

In that same village of Banneux in the year 1933 something happened that has put the village on the map as one of the main pilgrimage spots in Europe.

On some marshland about a mile from the village there lived a poor family by the name of Beco. With seven children to support and not much money coming in, it was a tremendous struggle trying to support the family. Although they were a Roman Catholic family, they had fallen away from their religion, and the children were not receiving catechism instruction, nor had they made their First Holy Communions.

One cold winter evening, the eldest child, eleven-year-old Mariette, was anxiously looking out of the window for a sign of her young brother, who was late home. Suddenly she thought she saw an odd light outside in the darkness. She assumed that the lamp in the window was creating some kind of reflection, so she moved the lamp into another room and returned to watch out for her brother. When she approached the window she stopped in her tracks when she saw that the light outside was still there.

On looking directly at the light which first appeared in the general shape of a person, young Mariette realized that she was looking at a beautiful young woman, dressed in white with a blue sash around her waist. Her dress reached to the ground and one foot was showing, upon which rested a golden rose. A rosary hung from her left arm. The natural reaction from Mariette was to run for her mother. Mme. Beco returned with her daughter to the window and she also saw something outside. To her it appeared as a light in the outline of a figure. She could not distinguish more than this, but Mariette then saw the young woman beckon her to go outside. At this point her mother refused to allow Mariette to go outside. On turning back towards the window, the vision had vanished.

The following evening at exactly the same time, 7.00 p.m., Mariette suddenly rose from her chair without saying a word to anyone and went outside. She was normally afraid of the dark, so her father followed her to see where she was going. He found the child kneeling on the frozen path, saying the rosary. Suddenly, Mariette raised her arms in the air. She told her father that she could see, far away up in the sky, the same vision of the young woman as she had seen the night before, but this time it was tiny. The figure in the sky grew slightly larger as it approached through the air and then came to rest on what appeared to be a small cloud quite close to Mariette about a foot above the ground.

The child was transfixed as she gazed at the vision. Her father was unable to distract her attention and so became quite worried. He realized he needed help and he got on his cycle to go to the village to fetch the priest. The priest was not at home, so M. Beco called upon one of his neighbours who returned with him to his own house, where they saw

51

Mariette coming out of the garden. The vision was beck-oning to the child in the same way as the night before. This time Mariette did follow, and called to her father, 'She is calling me.' About a hundred yards from the house the vision of the young woman, who was described as floating, turned, crossed the road and stood at a spot where a tiny spring trickled into a ditch. The woman spoke to Mariette saying to her, 'Plunge your hands into the water.' Mariet-te's father, his neighbour and his neighbour's young son watched Mariette kneel down and put her hands into the icy water as she repeated the woman's words, 'This spring is reserved for me.' Then the child said, 'Goodnight. Au revoir.' The woman then travelled upwards and back into the sky, growing smaller and smaller until she disappeared.

There were several more visions, all starting at exactly 7.00 p.m. and all arriving in the same way, from out of the sky at a great distance, then coming nearer to the child. On one occasion Mariette asked the lady, 'Who are you, Madame?' After a short pause, she was given the reply, 'I am the Virgin of the Poor.' In subsequent visions Mariette was told, 'This spring is reserved for all nations to relieve the sick.' The child became convinced that she had seen the Virgin Mary.

Mariette was questioned closely by her local priest, Father Jamin, who consulted Father del Marmol, O.S.B. They felt that the child had a vivid imagination and did not believe that she had seen the Virgin Mary. The family doctor examined the child, but could find no trace or evidence of pathological disturbance.

Since the apparitions the evening rosary, which the child started on the icy garden path, has been said each night at 7.00 p.m. in a little chapel which was built in the year of the visions. Pilgrims from all over the world pour into the unspoilt little village to visit the shrine and to bathe in the waters of the spring.

It was on one such pilgrimage that Fred, who travelled from Welwyn Garden City, was cured. He had been suffering from a bronchial condition which had weakened him so much that it was a strain just to go out of his house. His lungs kept filling up with pockets of fluid which had the same effect as pneumonia. He had been in and out of hospital for years and was constantly on pain-killing drugs. On his arrival at Banneux he was put straight into the hospital, thoroughly exhausted by the combination of pain and the long journey. The following evening he was taken to the spring.

'I had my hands in the water, as did my helper. He complained that the water was extremely cold, but I could not imagine why he said that. I distinctly felt the water warm. He immediately put this down to the possibility of me having a temperature and took me straight back to my bed. I was supposed to take two lots of tablets for the pain and to help me sleep but, for some reason, I just forgot all about them that night.

'From that night I've never had to take another tablet and my illness just disappeared. The very next morning I was up helping the sick, pushing wheelchairs around and even lifting people in and out of their beds, and helping them to the spring. I had no pain whatsoever.

'On my return to England I was examined by my doctor who said that I was in good condition but, to be on the safe side, I should go back to him in six months for another check-up, unless, of course, I had problems in the meanwhile. I had no relapse and, for the first time, I was able to play with the children and I even took up judo and swimming.

'Our Lady said that she had come to Banneux to relieve the sick and that's exactly what she has done for me.'

Mr. Marks' Story

Healing comes in all sorts of unusual ways as in the case of Mr. Marks of Oxford, who had suffered badly from an injured elbow and had tried every tablet and medication possible, but without success. 'I went to bed one night and something made me wake up. I was aware of a man entering my room through the doorway. I jumped up in the bed, most alarmed, thinking that I was being burgled. I was quite terrified and really didn't known what to do. The tall man stood still for a moment and just stared at me. I noticed that he was carrying a small bag and thought to myself that the stranger must be going to fill the bag up with my belongings, although I had nothing of much value in the house. I then thought about my wallet which was in my jacket pocket. It occurred to me to try to make a dash for this but I was frightened in case I would awaken my wife.

'I noticed that there was something odd about the way the stranger was looking at me. He did not seem to be after anything and there was a sense of calm in the room.

'I thought I'd better get out of bed and face him, so I slipped my legs down on to the floor. I was worried about what my wife would think if she woke up and, although I didn't want to look away from the stranger in case he tried anything, I glanced back quickly to make sure that my wife was still asleep. You can imagine my amazement when I saw that not only was she asleep, but I was lying beside her in the bed. I just couldn't figure out what was happening. I

54

remember backing away from the bed into the opposite corner of the room and as I did this, the stranger approached the bed, put down his bag and knelt beside my sleeping body.

'I watched as the stranger lifted up the arm of my sleeping body. When he did this a strange brilliant light appeared, surrounding the physical arm, in the region of the elbow. The stranger opened his bag and I saw him take out a kind of clamp and hold it still, all the time the light remaining on the area. The rest of the room was dim.

'I was so staggered at what was happening before my eyes that I think I was beyond being afraid. I seemed to become acclimatized very quickly to the new condition. Somehow it seemed quite natural.

'The stranger continued to work on my elbow, then, after what seemed to me like only a few minutes, he took the clamp off and immediately the strong white light faded. The man put the clamp back in his bag and, without looking over at me in the corner, he left the room through the doorway as he had entered, without uttering a word.

'I then began to feel aware of the proximity of my physical body and the moment I found myself thinking of the other me still asleep in the bed, I started to glide across the room and slide into my body. The next thing I remember was wakening up in the morning and remembering everything so vividly. I asked my wife if she'd slept well, and she said she had but made no other remark, so I thought it best to leave it at that. I looked at my elbow, and was interested to find there was no mark there and absolutely no pain. I say interested rather than surprised because after what I'd seen the night before, it didn't really come as a great surprise to find that my elbow had been healed. Don't ask me how he did it though. I don't even know who he was. All I can say is that I've never had any trouble with it since.'

Mrs. Hawkins' Story

A similar out-of-the-body cure was experienced by Mrs. Hawkins of Merseyside. She had been suffering from pains in her legs and one night she felt restless, and could not settle down to sleep. 'I rose up from my bed and was startled to find there was a man and woman in the room beside me. They beckoned to me to follow them. I then realized, to my great shock, that my physical body was still lying on the bed beside my husband. We were both fast asleep. I started to feel calmer at that point and all sense of fear left me. I knew that I was meant to follow the people who appeared to me as friends although I did not recognize either of them.

'I followed them out of the house and was led to a place with large plate glass windows. They walked inside and sat down by the window. Another two men joined us, one of whom I noticed was dressed in bishop's clothes. The bishop and the lady sat to my right and the other two men sat opposite me. It was then that I became strongly aware of yet another presence behind me. I did not look round, but somehow I could sense that it was another man.

'I felt his arms around me and then he raised me up. I was being eased down on to a bed where white silken sheets were being smoothed out for me by three pairs of hands on each side. Although the hands were not connected to arms this did not seem to matter to me, and it did not frighten me in the least. It was as if they were happy to help. I know that sounds ridiculous, but that's how it was.

'I then saw another two men dressed in white coats enter

56

the room. At this point I started to feel nervous. Then I heard the presence behind me speak. A manly voice told me not to worry, that there was nothing to be afraid of. I then relaxed as I watched the two men in white coats inject my legs with needles. I have never had any trouble with my legs since.

'There is a rather strange tailpiece to this story inasmuch as my mother was in hospital at that time; she was dying of cancer. The following day I went to the hospital to visit her, and the first thing Mum told me was that she'd had her legs injected. This puzzled me, as this was never a treatment which was in the pipeline for my mother to have. On checking with the doctors, I was assured that no person had given my mother any injection whatsoever. However, my mother still insisted that she had had injections in the legs. She told me that she could still feel the needles in her legs, and that she's felt much better since.

'I just thought that my mother was imagining it all, but it was strange when I remembered the two men in the white coats. At that point I really didn't know what to make of it all.

'Shortly afterwards my mum died. On speaking to her doctor, I was told that just before the end they had, in fact, given mum an injection in her leg.'

Richard's Story

Richard was a drug addict who had served various prison sentences for grievous bodily harm. He had a bad accident, which resulted in him being unconscious for thirteen days. He was left with the entire right side of his body completely paralysed. Through the laying on of hands and through prayer he was cured physically and emotionally. To show

57

his thanks to God, he wrote the following poem, which has since been set to music:

Tears of Sorrow

Through tears of sorrow and tears of regret
I gazed at the road I had trod.
But those tears could not hide what I could not forget –
How it led me away from God.
Then one day I knelt down at an old rugged cross,
And heard God saying, "Come home".
So through old and lost ages I sing his praises
For the way of the cross led me home.
These lips that once whispered unspeakable things
Forever his praises shall sing.
And these eyes so unworthy shall some day behold
The face of my Saviour and King.
And I look ahead to the old rugged cross
And heard God saying, "You're home".

Bishop Graham's Comments on the Healing Force
Note that in the Old Testament, healing was always carried out by special people – the prophets Elijah, Elisha, etc. They were specially chosen by God and they knew it and so did their 'clients'. Obedience was important. Healing was usually by word and touch.

Joel, a later Old Testament prophet, said that eventually this gift (amongst others) by the power of the Holy Spirit would be 'poured out on all people... your sons and your daughters will prophesy, your young men will see visions and your old men will dream dreams...', there would be 'signs and wonders' (Joel 2: 28-32).

Jesus announced that he was the first one upon whom the

spirit had been poured and, quoting the Old Testament prophet Isaiah (61. 1, 2), Jesus said at Nazareth:

'The Spirit of the Lord is upon me, therefore He has annointed me to preach good news to the poor; He has sent me to proclaim freedom for the prisoners, and recovery of sight for the blind; to release the oppressed, to proclaim the year of the Lord's favour (a "jubilee").' (Luke 4: 18-19)

And duly he went about healing people. He used words of command, touch and occasionally saliva and mud. His disciples accompanied him. Then he gave them his authority to do the same and they reported back their success – this also involved annointing with oil.

After his crucifixion and resurrection he gave a general authority to all his followers: 'Go into the world, preach the gospel and heal the sick,' saying, 'they will place their hands on sick people, and they will get well.' (Mark 16: 18). Subsequently this is exactly what the early church did.

Here I mention the letter of St. James (James 5: 14-16). 'Is any one sick? He should call the elders (literally presbyters) of the church to pray over him and annoint him with oil in the name of the Lord. And the prayers offered in faith will make the sick person well; the Lord will raise him up. If he has sinned, he will be forgiven. Therefore, confess your sins to each other so that you may be healed. The prayer of a righteous man is powerful and effective.'

The church down the ages, in one way or another, has continued this healing tradition in prayer, laying on of hands and annointing (not necessarily all at the same time!)

Numerous examples can be given – look at the works of St. Francis of Assisi; St. Ignatius; Martin Luther; John Wesley. Then there are the mendicant friars and monks, the Order of St. John, the growth of hospitals, etc., and then perhaps more recently in this country (and elsewhere) a growing recovery of the realization that Jesus' authority still has power today.

Hence 'healing meetings' such as described in this chapter (Anne) and individual cases of healing (Sister May and the crippled boy, Richard). Some involved touch, some annointing, but all prayer.

Note that 'faith' is not an absolute requirement – it could be the faith of the person being healed (Quote: 'Your faith has made you whole...') or the faith of the friends bringing the person to be healed, or healing may succeed so that '...the power of God should be revealed'.

That 'non-Christians' might also have this 'gift' would be covered by the typical generosity of God! (Example: Jesus turned 120 gallons of water into wine at the Wedding Feast at Cana right at the end of the meal when they had only just run out of wine!)

Also Jesus' acknowledgement that those who would be 'saved' would not only be those who cry 'Lord Lord', but also those who do the will of God. Healing is part of the will of God in restoring wholeness to the created order.

The individual 'healer' has no power of his/her own but is acting as a channel for the power of God. Mary and Peter's book uses the term 'healing force' to cover part of what I mean by the 'power of God' in its external form.

chapter six

STRANGE FORCES AT WORK

When a baby cries a visitor to the household will look up anxiously to the young mother, expecting her to immediately dash towards the cot. Sometimes the mother may not exert herself, much to the disdain of the visitor.

"It's all right, Mrs. Jones. I know that cry. There's no problem."

"But don't you need to attend to him?"

"Of course," smiles the young mother calmly. "But it's not urgent, I can tell by the cry."

The mother-child relationship is uniquely telepathic. After all, the tiny baby has not yet learnt coherent speech, and it certainly can't write mum a note, yet the mother seems to know instinctively not only the needs of her child, but also the degree of urgency involved. This can be true even when the parent and offspring are separated by hundreds of miles. The same forces are often at work between twins, husbands and wives, and relations.

Very often when experiments have been set up to try to prove that thoughts really can travel, it has appeared that the results are nothing more than those which would normally be expected under the headings of chance, coincidence, law of averages, statistics, etc. The trouble with such experiments seems to be the aimlessness of the operation. The secret of achieving anything bordering on worthwhile evidence seems to lie in the root cause of the situation, the underlying need for motivation of the power of thought.

In other words, if there happens to be a telephone close at hand, why bother trying to send a message by thought wave to granny down in the West Country. It's a lot less bother just to dial the number.

The most convincing instances of telepathy or thought travel seem to take place when there is no telephone, no other means of communication, and a crucial state arises whereby contact must be made. In these circumstances it appears that our brains have inbuilt radar systems which can send out messages, either consciously or unconsciously, to a given target.

When a pebble is thrown into a pond we see first the splash, on impact, then the ripples on the water. What we do not see is the ripples caused in the air above the pond, but that does not mean that they do not exist.

Hardly anyone has escaped the strangely irritating sensation of *déjà vu*. We look at possible explanations and relate stories of people who have been able to describe in detail places they know they have never before been to. Is it in the genes? Is it the way in which one part of the brain receives and analyses information a fraction of a second faster than the other half, thus giving the impression of familiarity? Are we dipping into a pool of cosmic knowledge?

Nuala's Story

When Nuala Walshe was introduced to a tall, handsome, fair-haired Australian who was visiting her small, remote village in the rustic west of Ireland, she was delighted to meet the newcomer who proved to be like a breath of fresh air to the close-knit community where everyone had known each other from birth. Des, the Australian, who was staying with his relatives about two miles away from Nuala's cottage, formed a friendship with her, which speedily blossomed into what they both thought was love. Nuala had been brought up by her aunt since her mother died when she was only three.

'I was excitedly looking forward to my engagement day. On the great day, Des had been invited by my aunt to have tea. At the tea table, without thinking much about it, I produced a letter from my father who had been living in England for years and who had recently re-married. He had written to congratulate us on our forthcoming marriage and had invited us to England to visit him and his new wife, whom I had never met. I got the shock of my life when Des suddenly snatched the letter out of my hand and, in a fearful rage, he tore it to pieces before my eyes.

'The next moment the most frightening thing happened. Suddenly the room grew icy cold. I felt a strange cold draft behind me, then as I looked over at Des I became absolutely terrified because there, standing behind his chair, was the figure of a young dark-haired man, watching me with a strange, concerned look on his face. I froze with fear, unable to utter a word, hardly daring to breathe. In an instant, the man disappeared.

'I looked across at Des and realized that he had gone deathly white. His eyes were staring into space as if he were looking at something behind my chair. I was still in a state of shock myself, and I couldn't even speak to ask what was wrong. Suddenly he passed out and collapsed down on the floor.

'I was so frightened that I could not move from my chair. My aunt fetched some water for Des, who recovered consciousness. He was mumbling that he had just seen a ghost. He said that a woman had appeared behind my chair and had stared at him. He was able to describe the woman, saying that her hair was piled up on top of her head in a kind of bun. I was still speechless with fright, and didn't dare open my mouth to tell him what I had seen behind his chair.

'Quietly, my aunt went over to the dresser, and from a drawer, she took out a small box. She returned to the table, opened the box and took out a silver locket on a chain. Des told her that was the locket he had seen on the woman's neck. My aunt and I exchanged glances. We both knew that the locket had belonged to my mother. Once more my aunt went to the drawer and returned with an old photograph of my mother which had never before been shown to Des. He looked at it with a terrified expression, and told us it was the same woman. My fiancé had seen the ghost of my mother.

'Des got up to leave. I would normally have seen him off at the door, but I was so upset that my aunt insisted that it would be best if I went straight to bed to calm down, so Des left the cottage by himself. He later told me what happened to him. As he had walked up the long pathway to the gate, he had become aware of the cold atmosphere again, even though it was a beautiful, warm August day, and the sun was shining. As he had gone to open the gate, he stared in horror when he saw the bolt moving on its own, and the gate opening for him, as if bidding him to leave. In a panic, he ran to his car to start the two mile journey to the house of his relatives.

'As he drove away from the cottage, a woman loomed out in front of his car, as if from nowhere. He slammed on his brakes, then he went into a panic as he recognized the woman. It was my dead mother. She was holding out her hand and pointing into the distance, as if trying to tell him to go away.

'Des told me that he started up the car again, and as he

drove forward, my mother floated in front of his car, all the time gesturing to him to go away. By the time he had reached his destination he was sick with fear. He got out of the car, and to his great relief, the woman was nowhere to be seen. He made his way to the gate, where he was stopped in his tracks. Again he saw the gate open by itself. It took him all his courage to enter past the gate, and as he did so, the gate closed behind him of its own accord.

'The next day Des visited me to tell me that the engagement was off because he was certain that my departed mother was trying to frighten him away. Then he told me that he had arranged to travel back to Australia within the next few days.

'To get over the disappointment of my broken engagement, I decided to take my father up on his offer to visit him in England. I was in a rather tearful state when I arrived, but my dad and his new wife Betty gave me a sympathetic welcome. Betty made me feel very much at home straight away, and a bond of friendship was instantly formed between us. Later that evening there was a ring on the doorbell, and as Betty got up to answer it, she remarked that it would probably be her nephew Jim, who was due to call round to see her. I couldn't believe my eyes when Jim entered the room. He was the same young dark-haired man I had seen standing behind Des in my aunt's cottage. I was even more amazed when he smiled at me, his first words being, 'Haven't we met before some place?'

Redwing's Story
Ron Turner, a young British airman in the Second World War, was honourably discharged, having been badly wounded in action. He moved to the West Country with his

wife Ellen, where they bought a run-down tea-room which they redecorated themselves, and then subsequently opened to cater for servicemen providing them with good, inexpensive luncheons.

Ellen recalls, 'A crowd of American airmen became regular customers, and two young men in particular became great friends with Ron and I. One of the Americans, called Bill, had shocking red hair and so was nicknamed "Redwing". Although I was happily married to Ron, I was nevertheless attracted to Redwing, and I felt that the feeling was mutual. Redwing always used to whistle "The Girl I Left Behind Me" and he always sat in the same seat.

'One day, after the Americans had been away for several weeks, some of Redwing's friends entered the luncheon room without him. Instantly I knew that something terrible had happened to him. Sure enough, I learned that Redwing had been missing for some time, presumed dead.

'A few years later, after Ron had died, one Easter Sunday afternoon, I was busy working in the kitchen. I had just locked up the luncheon room, when I suddenly heard a familiar whistle coming from the dining area, "The Girl I Left Behind Me". I slowly walked towards the dining area where I could see an American airman sitting alone. I remember the feeling of joy I experienced as I recognized the bright red hair. It was Redwing. He had come back. I started to walk towards him, then I stopped dead in my tracks when I realized that he had suddenly disappeared. I looked everywhere around the tearoom for him, but he was nowhere to be found.

'From that moment I was certain that Redwing was alive and I started to make enquiries, only to find little encour-

66

agement. Later that year, one winter's day, I was throwing out some rubbish at the side of the building when I saw a man muffled up in a large scarf, with a huge hat pulled down over his eyes. He was standing at the front door, looking at the "Closed" sign. I called over to him, telling him that I had just closed. He just stood there, staring at me, saying nothing. There was something about him that made me feel sorry for him, so I told him that I could offer him a bowl of soup.

'I opened up the tearoom door, without paying too much attention to him, and I went into the kitchen to prepare the soup. Suddenly, I heard a tune being whistled, "The Girl I Left Behind Me". At first I froze, then I ran out and saw the man from the back. He had taken off his scarf and hat. I would have recognized that red hair anywhere. I called out "Redwing", and he turned round with an impish smile and winked at me.

'We fell into each other's arms, and he told me that he had been in a prisoner-of-war camp for years, after he had been shot down over the North Sea. I asked him if he had ever come back to the tearoom, but he assured me that he had not. Then he told me that at one point he had been so ill that he had nearly died. I asked him if it had been last Easter. Redwing looked at me in astonishment and silently nodded his head.'

Dr. Sturman's Story
One late afternoon when Dr. Sturman had just returned home after his calls which that day had been heavier than normal, because of the multiple ailments which usually hit his patients in the depths of the British winter, he heard a knock at the door.

67

'I opened my door to find a young girl of about 17 years of age standing there. She wore a child's school hat on her head, one made from straw, which was drenched through with the heavy rain. The girl was near to hysterics. She begged me to come urgently to visit her father, who had suddenly taken ill.

'I did not recognize the girl, and soon established that her father was not my patient. I tried to reason with her, advising her to go to her father's own doctor. The girl's persistent sobbing convinced me that I should visit the father to see what I could do.

'I followed the girl along a few streets as she led me to her house. On the way I remember her telling me that she was most concerned for her mother who would be completely forlorn should her father die. Not knowing the extent of her father's illness I answered as sympathetically as I could, and I assured her that I would do what I could to help.

'On the way to the girl's house we passed a workmen's hut on the pavement. I remember that we had to walk past in the gutter as there was a burning brazier on the footpath. As we passed, I glanced into the hut where three workmen were seated. We nodded to them and they acknowledged us.

'When we reached the house, the girl stood back, so I knocked on the door, which was opened by the lady of the house. She was most distressed and was weeping. I explained that I had come to see her husband. The woman led me upstairs, but on the way she tearfully told me that I was too late as her husband had died minutes before.

'I examined the body and confirmed that death had taken place. The woman then asked me how I had known to come to the house. Somewhat surprised at her question I remind-ded her that her own daughter had called to see me and had asked me to visit her father urgently. She was the one who had led me to the house. The woman's face grew deathly white, then she told me that their only daughter had died ten years earlier. She had been coming home from school and was knocked down by a car and killed outright.

'As I walked back to my own home in a somewhat dazed state, I passed the workmen's hut again. I stopped and asked the men inside if they had noticed me only a few minutes earlier when I had passed them with a young girl.

'All three workmen laughed, then one of them explained that they had seen me pass their hut but they had wondered why I had been talking to myself. They had seen only me; there had been no girl with me.'

Denise's Story

One desolate Christmas Eve a young woman, Denise, walked along a quiet street, engrossed in her own thoughts. 'I hesitated to look across towards a toyshop doorway, from where the strains of "Silent Night" were coming. I saw an old tramp, dressed in a tattered military coat, playing his violin. I remember seeing a brightly lit Christmas tree in the shop window, but I had no heart for anything that night.

'I arrived at my mother's home and just managed to summon up enough courage to tell her my news before I broke down in tears. I had just had a visit from a soldier friend of my husband to tell me that my husband, Joe, was missing, presumed dead. Joe had been serving in Northern Ireland. My family rallied round and tried to comfort me, but with little success, although I tried hard to keep up a brave front.

'Although my mother pleaded with me to stay at her

house that night I insisted on going home just in case there might be any more news about Joe. Later that night I was even more melancholy, and I missed my husband desperately. I feared that he must be dead as he would definitely have contacted me for Christmas. I looked at some photographs of Joe in his army uniform. Tearfully I went to bed.

'Later I was awakened by someone tapping at the door. I was frightened, but I got up and went to answer. I peeped through the curtain, and to my joy I saw Joe standing outside the house. I rushed to the door and welcomed him in. I sobbed with relief as we hugged each other. It was then that I noticed that the front of his heavy army coat was soaked with blood. I stared at him in horror and asked him what had happened, then I told him I would call the doctor at once. In a vague, far-off voice, he replied, "It's OK, it's all better now." He kissed me again, and I asked him if he wanted a drink, and again I suggested that I call a doctor. I went to help him off with his coat, but he slowly shook his head, moved towards me and held out his hand. I took his hand and he led me into the bedroom.

'The following morning I awoke and excitedly turned round towards Joe, only to find that his side of the bed was empty. I looked around the room, then I ran to telephone my mother. As I started to dial the number there was a loud knock on the outside door. I could see the outline of a soldier in uniform. My mother answered the telephone. Breathless with excitement I told her briefly on the phone that Joe was all right, but I had to go because he was at the door. I told my mother to hold on saying that he must have lost his key.

'I ran to answer the door, expecting to see Joe, but I was

70

taken aback when I saw his friend, Alan, standing there instead. I asked him into the house. Solemnly he handed me an official letter which I read. I cried out in disbelief, saying that it couldn't be true. Joe couldn't be dead. He was here last night. I told Alan that there must be some mistake. He was sympathetic and told me that I was suffering from shock. He confirmed the contents of the letter, stating quietly that Joe had been killed on Christmas Eve.

'I looked at the telephone receiver, which was still off the hook. I murmured to Alan that my mum was on the line. Alan picked up the receiver and broke the news to my mother.'

Joanna's Story
'As a young nurse, some years ago, I was having a tea-break with my friend, and we were chatting about the new houseman, an extremely good-looking young Scotsman, Dr. Robertson. The young doctors were usually the topic of conversation, and I remember that I was particularly smitten with Dr. Robertson, and I admitted that I was looking forward to my forthcoming night duty, hoping that I would get the opportunity to talk to him and get to know him better.

'A few nights later, in the middle of the night, the ward sister asked me to check a drip which was attached to an elderly male patient, Mr. Taylor, who was in a serious condition in a side room. I did what Sister told me, then I spoke quietly for a while to the patient, who was very emotional and nostalgic. This was not unusual and I had been trained to cope with the situation. He asked me if I had a boyfriend, then he went on to tell me that whatever happened in my life I should always do what I felt was right, no matter what other people might tell me.

'I left the room and walked along the corridor to report back to Sister, but on looking back I caught a glimpse of a nun entering Mr. Taylor's room. I mentioned this to Sister, who remarked that it must be one of the nuns from nearby St. Cecilia's convent. We all knew that the nuns often popped over during the night, especially if any of the patients were near the end. Sister and I then exchanged a few words regarding Mr. Taylor and we mentioned the fact that he never had any visitors. Sister told me that he was a bachelor and he had no relations left in this country, only a sister in Canada.

'Sister then asked me to put the kettle on to make some tea, and to remember to make a cup for Dr. Robertson. Before I had finished making the tea, Dr. Robertson came into the kitchen and we chatted for a few minutes. The doctor had just come from Mr. Taylor's room and, for the sake of conversation, I mentioned that I'd better get the nun a cup of tea as well. He asked me, "What nun?" I presumed she must have left.

'The following night, as I started night duty and the day nurses went off duty, I was told to keep a special eye on Mr. Taylor, so I went along to speak to him. I noticed that he was much weaker than before. Trying to cheer him up, I asked him if his visitor would be coming back to see him. He replied that he had never had a single visitor since he had arrived at the hospital. I assumed that he must have fallen asleep the night before when the nun had visited him. He raved on a little about how he could have had a family if only he'd not listened to others. He then dozed off to sleep and I left the room.

'I was walking along the darkened corridor when something caught the corner of my eye. I looked round just in time to see the nun enter Mr. Taylor's room. I went straight to Sister's office where Dr. Robertson was discussing a patient. I told them that I just wanted to mention that I had just seen the nun go into Mr. Taylor's room again. Dr. Robertson then decided he would go and check Mr. Taylor, and Sister nodded to me to go with him.

'We walked quietly down the long dark corridor until we reached the door of Mr. Taylor's room, from where we could see the nun standing at the end of his bed. At this point she had her back to us. Dr. Robertson gave a quiet cough, then we entered the room. The doctor glanced at Mr. Taylor, who appeared to be asleep, then he turned to the nun. For the first time I saw the nun's face. She was young and very beautiful. Dr. Robertson remarked quietly that Mr. Taylor had settled down all right. The nun smiled very sweetly and said, "I'll look after him now." With these words she turned to leave the room.

'I suddenly screamed out in terror, "She's got no feet!" Dr. Robertson glanced down just in time to see the nun glide out of the room, her long robes almost touching the ground, but not quite. I knew he had seen the same as me. His eyes widened in fear as he realized that I was right, the nun had no feet! I was shaking with fear. Dr. Robertson rushed towards me and put his arms around me to comfort me. We both walked quickly out of the room to have another look at the nun. When we got to the corridor it was completely empty and the nun had disappeared. We immediately went back into the room to check Mr. Taylor, and we found that he was lying in the bed, dead.

'Later, when we were going through Mr. Taylor's locker,

I came across an old poetry book. As I lifted it up, a photograph fell out on to the floor. My heart jumped with fright as I recognized the girl in the photograph. It must have been taken when Mr. Taylor was a young man. He was laughing cheerfully, with his arm round the pretty blonde girl in a flowered summer dress. There was no mistaking her face. It was the nun who had come back for him after all these years. I couldn't help the tears rolling down my cheeks.'

chapter seven

ANIMALS

What is the difference between human beings and animals? As far as their physical bodies are concerned there is no difference other than those arising from culture. The flesh, blood and bones of an animal are comprised of the same atoms and molecules as those of the human body. The structure and assembly of these particles decree the form, shape and species of the resultant living being, the blueprint.

It has been stated by various religions that what makes animals different to human beings is the fact that they have no souls. This would appear to be an over-simplification. Although the animal does not seem to have a soul similar in nature and origin to that of the human being, it does not necessarily follow that there is no soul. In fact, evidence suggests that animals do survive physical death.

Perhaps the differences between animals and humans can be described as follows: human beings have a spirit which, on physical death, rises towards its own natural sphere of existence, depending on the development of the spirit at that point in its evolution towards its optimum state of perfection. Animals, on the other hand, merely move on to their own animalistic realm on physical death.

It appears that animals are especially susceptible to mystic forces. It is well documented that an animal will react in a frightened manner when it is taken to certain locations and, in fact, it is often the reaction of an animal which draws attention to the fact that something odd has occurred at a particular spot. Many old English pubs have rooms where the owner's dog refuses to enter. Often we find that people report feeling a chilled atmosphere in such rooms, even though the central heating is operating at full capacity.

One particular pub in Northamptonshire is, to all appearances, trying to fight against being renovated. The chief architect (working on behalf of a major brewery) reports that since he started work on the site several months ago, every task which would normally be completed without any problems seems to be fraught with difficulties, without any logical reason. They have had a record number of injuries on site, and the morale of the workmen is at an all-time low. The project is under such stress that it is, in fact, in danger of being cancelled. Perhaps it is only coincidence, but this particular pub was used as a shelter for dying soldiers from the battle of Naseby. Rather than allow the men to die on the open field, they were carried in and stretched out in the cellar. All of the men died in that room. And now, over three hundred years later, the present landlord cannot entice his two Alsatian dogs into the cellar under any circumstances, yet the dogs roam freely throughout the rest of the building. Could it be that vibrations from that battle are still felt in the vicinity?

The suffering of the soldiers seems to be lingering on in the vibrations surrounding the pub, and these are picked up by the animals. These forces are so negative that they are not conducive to the type of plan that the brewery is trying to execute for that building.

Another example of an animal reacting to negative vibrations is given by Mrs. Mylak of Daventry who reports that the morning after Halloween she and her dog started their usual morning walk. 'Suddenly, the dog stopped dead

76

in his tracks. His hair stood up, from the top of his head to his tail. The skin on his face was tight, he was scared stiff. I bent down to his level, but could see nothing. I took him home, or rather he took me. Once he had calmed down, I took him again on the same path, and exactly the same thing happened at the same spot. By this time I was glad to go home with him, as I felt as scared as he looked. An hour later he took the path with my husband, and he walked on, perfectly normal.'

Mr. Turner of Kent reports a similar occurrence. He used to take his Alsatian dog on a regular early morning walk. 'It was very dark at the top of the road leading into the field. Every morning four local ladies would meet and go along a path by the field to a nearby school where they were cleaners. This particular morning, as I went into the field, they were walking along the path about thirty yards from me. One was shining her torch and they were chatting to one another when, all of a sudden, the whole field was lit up by the whitest light I have ever seen. It was brighter than daylight. I looked up, expecting to see a flare, but there was nothing in the sky to account for it. I could see the ladies going by, but they did not seem to see the light. They never even looked up, in fact the one with the torch was still shining it on the ground as they went along. My dog had gone down on his belly and was whimpering with fright. This lasted only a few seconds, and then it all went dark. The next day I saw the ladies and asked them about the light, but they had seen nothing. This never happened again, but for a long time afterwards I had a job to get my dog to go into that field.'

Sometimes, although there is no evidence of anything traumatic having occurred in a specific location, phantom animals are sighted, as in the case of a lady from Northamptonshire:

'One Saturday night, around 7.45 p.m. my husband, myself and our son, then aged five, were travelling in the car along the A509 from Wollaston to Bozeat. It had been snowing, just enough to cover the fields and verges with a thin layer. Just as we were approaching a spot called Fullwell Hill we noticed the large silhouette of a dog. I say silhouette as this is how it appeared at the time. It appeared to get closer to the road as it ran and, at one point, a huge shadow seemed to pass through the right side of the car. It all happened so unexpectedly, and we did not think it weird at that moment. We assumed it had got loose from one of the farms and the snow was causing the shadow effect. For a short time we lost sight of it, but suddenly we could make out the dog's figure against the snow as it came from the hedge towards the road a few yards in front of us. My husband braked, but the dog just disappeared as it reached the middle of the road.

'Nothing could have been further from my mind than ghosts until that moment, when I realized that we had seen the phantom dog that I had heard talked about many years before, and that was said to appear at that very spot. Strangely, when the dog came out into the road it appeared a normal size border collie, but it looked like the negative of a film. I could clearly make out the markings and shape, but there was no real substance. If it had been a real live dog our car would have hit it.

'I have since been told by a young man that he has also seen the dog, whilst he was travelling along the same stretch of road on his motorbike.'

A new bypass has recently been built, which covers the

78

spot where this lady first saw the dog, and it will be interesting to note if any further sightings are made.

Another version of the phantom animal is contained in a report from Ted of Luton, but this time it occurred at the moment of the dog's death.

'Pip was an old dog, suffering very badly from arthritis. Her back legs were stiff, and if she was lying down she would give a low growl and I would have to pick her up and put her on her feet. Eventually things got so bad for her that I decided to have her put down, and took her to the vet.

'I stood her up on the operating table, while the vet prepared the syringe. He took a long time over his preparations to give me time to change my mind. I looked at Pip's face, she looked me straight in the eye, and I felt a real coward for doing this to her, although she was in pain. I had to avert my eyes from her gaze. She seemed to be saying "Why?" to me.

'Within a few seconds the vet had injected her and she died, although there was no change, she just stood there, supported by me. I looked at ther and did not think she was dead. The vet said, "It's OK, she's gone now."

'I moved over to the desk to write out the cheque and the vet turned away to wash his hands. I turned to look at Pip lying on the table, when suddenly I saw what seemed to be a young version of Pip coming from her head. It was just as solid as the corpse, and was lying in the same position. It seemed to glide, and made a right hand turn just before the end of the table, at the point where the vet normally stood. As it moved towards the side of the table I saw a pair of hands in what looked like a monk's brown habit appear to receive it. The dog's head seemed to disappear into an aperture, followed by the strange hands and the rest of the dog's body. I looked back at the table to see Pip still lying there. The whole thing took about four to five seconds.'

An interesting point arises from this story that if animals could speak, perhaps they would report experiencing out-of-body travels, and it would be fascinating to compare their accounts with those of human beings. If animals are connected to the astral world in the same way as humans, i.e. by a cord of some description, then the theory is that as long as the cord remains unsevered, the spiritual body can come back and be reunited with the physical one. When the cord is broken, permanent death takes place.

The healing forces are not exclusive to human beings and can be used to great effect to cure animals. A lady from New Zealand, who was already well known as a dowser, or water diviner, discovered that she could adapt this particular ability for healing both human beings and animals. She became a human conductor and attracted the healing forces towards the patient. She treated a race horse who had hit a hurdle, severly bruising its chest. She was asked to treat it, as a last resort, and it recovered to win again.

Perhaps wishes are granted in the afterlife, as in the case of the gentleman from Kent, who had always wanted to have a dovecote in his garden. His widow reports that, 'I disagreed as being in a built-up area I said we would have complaints from the neighbours about the cooing. After his death my mother stayed with me for a while. Imagine my surprise one day when looking out of the window I saw two white doves in the garden. We had never seen doves in the garden before. I remarked to my mother how thrilled my husband would have been to have seen them. One evening shortly afterwards, I had my bedroom windows open as it was very hot. When I went to close the windows I spotted a white dove sitting on a shelf over the window. I couldn't get it down, so I called my neighbour, who told me that he had seen the dove sitting in my open window all evening. My neighbour had a great deal of trouble in putting the dove out, as it seemed reluctant to go. Before going to bed that night, I went into another bedroom to draw the curtains, and there was the dove, sitting on the outside of the window ledge. I remained in the house another two years, but never saw doves again.'

Perhaps old wives' warnings cannot be laughed off so easily when we hear such tales as the magpies of Chippenham, Wiltshire, which appeared to give a definite warning of impending death. Mrs. Hughes says, 'Our lounge, living room and bedroom windows look out onto our field garden, as we call it. There used to be two magpies which regularly sat on the field fence. One morning one of these magpies woke up my husband and myself by pecking viciously on our bedroom window. The look in its eyes was quite alarming. I knew that tits pecked at the insects on windows, but had never known magpies to do this.

'About an hour later we received a phone call to tell us that my mother-in-law had died. This came as a great shock as although she was in hospital she was expected home the following day, as she had recovered. My husband, who is not at all superstitious says that he had heard this old country tale many times, but had never believed it. This happened two years ago, and although we still have magpies in our garden, they have not pecked at the window since.'

Animals feature in different types of psychic phenomena, including unusual or prophetic dreams and telepathy, There are lots of examples of people being in telepathic communication with their pets. Mrs. Hague relates that she had to go to Africa, and while she was away from home she had asked a kindly neighbour to look after her cat. On her way back from Kenya she had a vivid dream that her cat was being offered a saucer of milk from a stranger. Something about the expression on the cat's face worried her. She suddenly became aware of the fact that this was no ordinary saucer of milk. 'It was as if a voice in my head was telling me that the milk had been poisoned.' Throughout the long journey home she was worried about the cat and could not get it out of her mind.

The most upsetting aspect of the dream was that although she knew that the animal was being offered poisoned milk, she was totally helpless and could do absolutely nothing to prevent her cat from drinking the milk.

As soon as she arrived home she went to her neighbour and was greeted with a sorrowful story. The cat had become unaccountably ill, and the neighbour had taken it to be put down.

It often happens that when a death takes place in a family, the animals of the dead person react in strange ways, possibly because they are more aware of vibrations in the ethereal sphere.

Mrs. Newman of Hampshire experienced this when her mother died suddenly, leaving the entire family grief-stricken. 'My sister and husband, my brother and wife, my daughter, my husband and I were working out mother's papers on the following Tuesday in my house. Suddenly the phone rang. I answered it. A good friend was phoning with her condolences. I chattered away, saying how much this friend had always cheered me up.

82

'Looking across the room, past the family gathered round the table, I saw over the curtains, towards the farthest corner of the room, a bright orange ball. For some reason I watched it without bringing the attention of the family to it. The cat suddenly started to behave very oddly. She rushed to the curtains, then under the table, back to the curtains looking very frightened, eyes wide and ears back. I excused myself from the friend on the phone, mentioning the behaviour of the cat. My husband and I went to the windows to see if anyone was outside. We opened the door, but the cat wouldn't go out.

'Within ten minutes all was calm again. The cat had quietened down and, of course, by then I had forgotten the light, it had vanished. Later, sitting relaxed in the lounge, my brother remarked, "Mum has been here tonight." We all agreed, feeling that she had been to see that we were all all right and once having satisfied herself she went. I discussed this with the vicar, who had heard of similar stories.'

Sometimes, the opposite happens. When the animal dies, the owners report that their pets come back to visit them. These feelings are very strong and cannot easily be talked away. The most common example is the sensation of the animal's fur rubbing against the master's legs. Sometimes, if the animal had a particular cushion upon which it always rested, the bereaved owners would see the cushion incline as if the animal were still sitting there, although usually no visible trace of the animal is reported.

In some cases sounds are perceived, not always in the obvious way, such as a dog's bark or a cat's meow, but in more subtle ways such as the sound of claws scraping on a door in exactly the same way as the pet used to scrape when it was alive. Perhaps the reason for this is that a straightforward bark might not be sufficiently distinctive and, indeed, might be lost to the perception of the owner, especially if there were other dogs in the vicinity. Usually these 'messages' come in such a way as to leave the owner in no doubt whatsoever that their own pet has been trying to make contact by using a method of communication peculiar to that individual pet.

For example, a listener to Birmingham's Radio WM reported that he had lost his dog and immediately bought another one. However, the new dog was very different in its habits to the one which passed over. The dead animal had always scraped on the door in a distinctive manner. It would only give one long scrape. The new dog used to scrape ferociously at the door with a repetitive action, not stopping until the door was opened. On various occasions, the owner distinctly heard the sound of the dead dog's one long scrape on the door.

'At first I didn't think anything of it, assuming that it was my new dog. I suppose I'd been so used to hearing the single long scrape for so many years that I was more or less seasoned to it. One particular night I heard the long solitary scrape sound, I got up to let, as I thought, the new dog in, and I was taken aback when my new dog came running along behind me. It had been inside in the kitchen towards the back of the house, in a completely different direction. I bent down to stroke my new dog and, at that moment, I heard the solitary scrape again. I remember looking at my new dog in amazement, wondering how on earth he could be standing beside me and scraping outside the door at the same time. It was only at that point that it dawned on me that, of course, the long scrape was how my dead dog used

to tell me that he wanted to be let into the house. I naturally
went the few paces to the door, opened it, but I could see
nothing. I smiled to myself at the time, thinking what a
rascal my dead dog was, giving me a turn like that. The
strange thing is that as soon as I accepted in my heart that
the old dog had tried to communicate with me, I never
heard his scrape again. It was as if he had made his point
and he was now happy to leave it at that.'

chapter eight

MUSIC

One point which keeps arising time and time again during our research of cases of out-of-body experiences is in connection with music. Not just the ordinary sounds of earthly music, but something much more – something that defies description in our earthly vocabulary. Most people end up by using the term 'Heavenly Music'.

The manner in which the music becomes evident to people varies considerably. Sometimes it is heard as a beautiful melody, sometimes there are pure voices heard singing in unknown tongues, sometimes the music is the trigger which switches people into another dimension, or often it is the vehicle whereby the attention is drawn to the fact that something strange is taking place.

A man was in Co. Sligo in Ireland, on holiday from Zimbabwe with his sister and her husband. They were walking across a remote field towards a lone cottage which stood by the shore, when suddenly, as if from out of the sky, a blast of joyful music echoed across the field. There was no sign of anyone else in the area. They both heard it and were afraid. The husband reported:

'It was an unnatural fear, that I have never experienced before and never want to again. I could feel the hairs on the top of my head stand erect. I could see that my wife was terrified, so I told her to pay no heed and just keep walking.'

The music seemed to follow them. They quickened their steps, but still the music seemed to be with them.

They then became aware that the nature of the music changed slightly as if a girl soloist was being featured, a clear, high-pitched, ringing voice singing in a foreign language. As soon as the girl's voice was heard, the woman turned to her husband and said, 'It's Mary!'

Mary had been married to the woman's brother, with whom they were on holiday, but she had died twelve years previously during the birth of their son. She was Dutch. Afraid to tell his brother what had happened for fear of upsetting him, the woman reported the story to the authors the day after she had heard the music, saying that she was worried about her brother. She had the feeling that the music seemed connected with him, as if it were 'calling' him. He was a fit man, in his prime, with three sons on holiday with him, and a daughter back in Africa. Within a week the man was dead. He had suffered a dreadful head injury from a fall, was rushed to hospital and died within hours.

A young boy of 14 skipped school one day. He saw a horse and cart approaching, and thought he would go closer. The horse kicked him, and he fell down, one of the wheels of the cart running over his arm. The next thing he knew, he was hovering above, looking down on his body which was lying on the ground. He became surrounded by a brilliant light and heard the most joyous, high-pitched music. 'It was so beautiful and made such an impression on me that I was unable to speak about it to anyone for years.'

A lady from Norwich reports that, 'One Good Friday I was part of a congregation singing "Sing My Tongue The Glorious Battle". I found I was about a foot in front of myself and a little higher up, and could hear myself singing behind me. When the hymn was finished, and I "fell into place", I felt cold. Of course it is an emotional time, and I was hungry – this may be relevant. I think the anonymous composer knew very well what he was doing! I have been on the edge of being "sent" before and since, but this is the only time I have been right over.'

Another example of church music having an effect comes from Aberdeen, where a lady reports, 'Many years ago, I was standing singing in the church choir, when suddenly my soul (or spirit) left my body. I went floating up past the pulpit but then thought, "What if my body doesn't sit down at the end of the hymn?" So, I willed myself back into my body, with a jerk. I was in perfect health at the time.'

Music can be used as a warning in some instances and often can come to the rescue of vulnerable people who cannot help themselves. A very disturbing story was related by a young girl, who had been brought up in New York, and who was unfortunately a victim of child battering.

The mother used the child as a scapegoat whenever there were problems, and the result was that the child lived in a constant state of fear. On one particular day, while she was suffering physical violence from her mother, suddenly the piano which stood in the corner of the room started to play of its own accord. The tune was distinctive as being the only one played by the child's aunt, who had recently died.

'There was no mistaking the tune, and my mother stopped beating me instantly as we both stared in amazement at the piano. We could definitely see the keys moving up and down, as if they were being depressed by unseen fingers. There is no doubt in either of our minds that my aunt was making her presence felt, and from that day on my mother never mistreated me again and, in fact, we became good friends.'

In some cases the origin of the music is fairly easily

traced, as in the case of a woman who lived in the top flat of an old house with her husband and new baby. She was very fond of music, but did not own a piano.

From time to time she was invited down to the ground floor flat by an elderly lady, whose late husband had been a professional pianist and who had, in fact, played at Carnegie Hall. The man had recently died, and the old lady enjoyed the company of the young woman and her baby.

'One day I tried to play "I'll Find You". Suddenly I felt as if someone was watching me. Then I sensed someone moving my fingers onto the right notes. I was absolutely petrified. The old lady was not in the least perturbed – she simply smiled and said, "That's my husband, trying to teach you."'

When author, George Chaplin, was researching his book on the famous composer, Lawrence Wright, a strange thing happened that he cannot explain. He went to Blackpool to the house of the late composer to interview his house-keeper, in order to get some background information on the man.

The house was called 'Souvenirs' after one of his famous songs 'Among My Souvenirs'. The interview went very well, and as Mr. Chaplin was about to leave, the house-keeper suggested with a laugh that she should give him her rendering of 'Among My Souvenirs' on the old piano, which had belonged to the composer. The author turned on his tape recorder, and the housekeeper played it through. When Mr. Chaplin played it back, he felt that he should have been a little closer to the piano as the recording was not as clear as it might have been. He suggested that the housekeeper play it through again, and that he would try to obtain a better recording. From that moment on, the tape recorder would not function, no matter which buttons he pressed. The housekeeper just laughed, and said, 'Lawrie's up to his tricks again. He wants you to keep the version I have played. Just wait and see – as soon as you leave the house your tape recorder will be fine.' When Mr. Chaplin left 'Souvenirs', he thought he would turn the tape recorder on to see what would happen. Sure enough, it played as normal.

chapter nine

BORDERLAND

There are varying accounts of the scenic surroundings encountered during out-of-the-body excursions. There does seem to be a united opinion that the wandering spirit reaches an area which can be described as a 'Borderland', situated at the demarcation line between the two realms of consciousness. This borderland lies within the area of brilliant light so often encountered, and is always described as being unbelievably tranquil. In fact, most people state quite clearly that they would have preferred to stay with the beneficial effects of the borderland, rather than return to their earthly bodies for all sorts of reasons. The moment the will to return becomes uppermost in their minds, they are instantly drawn back and into their physical bodies.

In some instances people find that they have to put up a tremendous struggle to return to their bodies, always with the terrifying thought that if they do not manage to get back they will be dead. Other people report that they are more or less ordered to go back because the time has not yet come for them to pass over.

While in hospital after a serious accident, Mr. Stephenson of Lincoln floated out of his body. He felt a great freedom and enjoyed the weightlessness as he travelled towards an earthly coloured valley. 'I came to a beautiful silver stream which, although fast flowing, sounded quiet and it had a strange calming effect on me. Across the stream on the far bank was the greenest grass I've ever seen. There was a hill, on top of which stood a huge, solitary tree. Behind the tree was the most brilliant light you could imagine. There is no earthly brilliance to compare it with. Our sun seemed like a dim candle glow in comparison to this wonderful light.

'At this point, I became aware of the voice of my minister, who was praying and calling on God to save me on behalf of my wife and small family. All I could think of at that moment was how much I dearly longed to cross the stream and reach the other side, to the beautiful peace. As much as I tried to approach the edge of the water, something seemed to be holding me back. Again I could hear the minister's voice, pleading for my recovery. I was truly disappointed at the thought of having to leave such beauty and comfort. The third prayer by the minister asked God to remember Mrs. Stephenson and her small family. Something must have clicked when I heard those words, for the next moment I found myself back in my hospital bed. I was quite angry, and I remember snapping at the nurse, asking her whatever was going on; I did not wish ever to come back here – why didn't he (the minister) leave me alone?'

The Sister in charge of the ward came up to Mr. Stephenson and told him quite frankly that there were very grave fears for him ever getting better. He felt so rejuvenated after the experience that he laughed at the idea, and told the Sister that he would be up in a few days. Sure enough, much to the surprise and wonderment of the staff, he was out of bed in three days.

Many people see gates of different kinds, which mark the boundary into the afterlife. A Wirral lass encountered beautiful pearl gates, and she recognized lots of people she knew, who had all died, standing around with open arms as if to welcome her. It was a moving sight, full of all the love that the people could pour down on her.

When a lady of Preston, Lancashire, was taking a casual stroll one day, she felt her spirit body walk out in front of her physical one. 'I stepped into a silent world of filmy mist. I found myself in a dark, damp tunnel and there, far ahead, was a brilliant small light which grew bigger and bigger. I then noticed a white wicker gate, but as I put my hand out to open it I heard a voice telling me to halt. There, before my eyes, I saw my dead father, who was sitting on a marble seat, looking well and young. He said, "You go back and tell your mother that at last I am happy." The garden in which he sat was glorious, with all the flowers one could find.'

Peter Hall, from Cambridge, described what happened to him. 'I cannot remember leaving my body, but I became suddenly aware that I was floating in my room in hospital. I was near the ceiling by the door of the room, and was looking down at myself lying on the bed. I could see all the tubes attached to me and the traction on my legs. I then floated out of the room and found myself walking in a strange place. It was hot sunny weather, and I was walking on sand. Ahead of me I could see a very high wall with no windows in it. I would estimate that it would have been in excess of twenty feet high. The only break in the wall was a pair of large wooden gates. I went straight up to the gates to see if there were any gaps in the wood, so that I could look through them to see what was on the other side. There were no gaps so I started to knock on the gates. Because the wood was so thick I realised that no-one would hear my feeble knocking, so I started pounding on the gate with my fist. Someone from behind the gates called out to me, "Peter, you can't come in – go back where you came from."

93

I couldn't see anyone so I looked around behind me and I got the shock of my life when I saw myself lying in the hospital bed again, with a doctor leaning over me. The ward sister was by his side. I seemed to gently slide back into my physical body, and when I opened my eyes I saw the doctor's anxious face staring down at me.

'Nothing was said; they turned and walked away, and I stayed where I was. I have never experienced anything like it before or since. It was as if I was dying, and when I was sent back by that voice it was decided that I should live.'

A lady of Armagh, Northern Ireland, came across a wooden gate when she was in labour. She was having a rough time, and she knew that the birth of her child was imminent. 'Just at the last moment, before my son came into the world, I had the feeling of travelling down a very dark, long corridor. I was approaching a bright light, which seemed to be at the far end of the corridor. As I drew nearer to the light I saw the most beautiful garden of golden daffodils. There was an ordinary wooden gate, and I could sense that there was someone standing at this, although I could not actually see anyone. I was not allowed to enter the gate and I could hear someone calling me back. I turned away from the gate very reluctantly, and heard someone calling my name, and then I felt someone's hand touch my face. I opened my eyes to find that it had been the nurse's voice I heard calling my name, and she was soothing my forehead. I have often wondered since what it would have been like to go through that gate, and indeed at the time I had a strong longing to do so. Only for the fact that I had just given birth to my baby son, I didn't.'

Flowers of all descriptions are seen at the Borderland. Ann Barrett from Kent, remembers what happened when she was attending a memorial service in the Crematorium Chapel at Charing in Kent. 'A very dear friend called Marguerite was being cremated. I was alone, but there were many mourners there. I was singing a hymn, and suddenly I wasn't there at all. I was standing in an open doorway looking across a lovely field fringed with trees. It appeared to be high summer, and the grass in the field was a vivid shade of green, lush, about six to nine inches high, and covered in marguerites. I could see every individual flower moving although, of course, there were hundreds and hundreds. Suddenly, breathlessly, I was back in the pew in the chapel, still singing, but we were about four lines of the hymn further on.

'I gave a quick glance round, but all was just the same as I had left it.

'This all happened several years ago, but the beauty, clarity and fresh perfection of every detail has not faded in the slightest. I have always lived in the country, but I have never seen a field like this before or since.'

Another example of an out-of-the-body experience during childbirth comes from Christine of Bedford, who found herself going down a dark tunnel, at the end of which was a light. 'I entered into this light and found myself in a most beautiful area of grass and trees, which was so peaceful and welcoming. The colours were so much more vivid and clear than anything I have seen before. Suddenly, I appeared to be above my body, hovering on the ceiling, watching myself lying on the bed.'

A more elaborate description of the boundary territory comes from Olive Wright of Gateshead, Co. Durham. 'I was being transported at a tremendous speed through mid-air, then I found myself lying on a marble slab inside what looked like a brilliantly lit castle. As I looked up, there was a man wearing a sort of Roman-type clothing. He had a very concerned expression and he started to press down on my stomach. I looked around the room and I could see other men, similarly dressed, attending to other people who were also stretched out on slabs. As these men walked about, I could hear their footsteps echoing through the castle hall or whatever it was. The next thing I was back in my own bed.'

A woman from the north of England sent us the following account of what happened to her departed grandfather over a century ago.

'A miracle of prayer came to me in 1888 when I had the ordeal of seeing my own body and coffin and thanks to the Rev. Thomas Mason of Deptford Church, Sunderland, I am now 72 years and five months, and can still record what I went through in 1888.

'One day I came in from work and lay down on the sofa for a few minutes before dinner. All of a sudden everything went black – as if I was on a train entering a tunnel – and I felt as if I was floating upwards. I saw quite clearly my landlady come in, find me lying there and send for the doctor. He put his instrument on my chest, and actually wrote out my death certificate. The next thing I remember I was back in the tunnel where I was met by a guide, who was exactly in the form of a human being. He said to me, "Look neither to the right nor to the left, but follow me." And he led me on to a point of light I could see in the distance. But I could not restrain my curiosity and looked down on my left, where I saw an immense gulf filled with countless people, among whom I recognized quite clearly pals of mine who had already died.

'Suddenly we emerged on to a wide plain, whose beauty I cannot describe. There were grass and trees and flowers as on earth, but of no earthly loveliness. And from there I saw a city as of alabaster with towers and turrets, and a little door where only one might enter at a time. After prayer we entered, and inside I was at once greeted by my father and mother whom I had never known for they had died when I was very young.

'My guide led me towards the Figure and the crowd parted to make way for us. When we arrived before Him my guide stood aside, and Jesus received me into His arms and blessed me. Then Jesus turned back to my guide and said, "Take him back to earth until his work be done." And the guide took me back to the gate whereby we had entered and left me. Immediately all went dark again.

'I awoke on my bed, all bound up and with my arms crossed on my chest. By the fireside I clearly saw my coffin. The minister, who was beside, me, had seem a small vein throb in my forehead and had sent for the doctor. I then saw them desperately trying to hide the coffin from me – but it was too late.

'When I woke, I am told that I wept for two hours for the beauty I had left.'

chapter ten

TIMESLIPS

In the days before electric light was in common use a man called Frederick lay in bed, reading by the glow of a little candle which flickered on a small table by his bedside. He grew tired, put the candle out, and fell fast asleep. He had the most wonderful dream in which he saw himself as a little boy, running around his parents' home, playing make-believe battles with his toy soldiers. He relived his childhood days, step by step, through his schooling, then remembered how he had felt the first time he'd kissed his sweetheart.

As a young man Frederick was then called to action, and with a stout heart and a prayer he set off to fight in the Napoleonic Wars. No longer did he face tin soldiers; now it was for real. He remembered clearly the look of terror in the eyes of the first man he had ever killed, the man he had been indoctrinated to believe was his enemy. He looked just like any other human being, he did not appear evil or have two heads!

As the fatal blow was struck, the impact affected not only the victim. For years and years the face of that dying man haunted Frederick's mind. He tried hard to make sense of it all.

One day, shortly after he returned home safely from the war, he met a young girl called Florence. She had a sunny disposition and Frederick slowly but surely fell deeply in love with her. He was overjoyed when he learnt that the feeling was mutual. He approached her father and formally asked for her hand in marriage. The happy event took place and the couple went off on their honeymoon to Sorrento on the west coast of Italy.

They were out one afternoon walking and enjoying the sights when Frederick's hat blew off. Florence's instant reaction was to run after it. Just as she reached out, the hat disappeared over the edge of a deep chasm. Frederick's heart missed a beat as he watched his beloved Florence stumble and lose her balance. With every ounce of energy he could muster he threw himself forward and landed bodily on top of Florence's legs, pinning her to the ground. She froze with fear as the entire top half of her body hung over the edge of the fissure. Onlookers came quickly to the rescue and pulled Florence up to safety. Frederick held her in his arms until she stopped shaking.

Shortly after they returned from Italy, Frederick was given a partnership in his uncle's firm, running a small newspaper, and he was able to buy Florence a beautiful house in Richmond, Surrey, near to the banks of the Thames. Life was beautiful and they were deliriously happy. Nothing could be more wonderful, thought Frederick, until Florence came to him, beaming radiantly with the news that she was expecting a baby'

Little Susannah came into the world on a bleak December day, just before Christmas. Frederick always remembered that first Christmas with his new daughter as one of the most wonderful, peaceful times in his life. Other children followed, three sons and another daughter.

The boys were very different in character, but Philip, the middle son, always displayed a marked flair for business. All of the boys were educated at Eton, went on to University and followed different careers. The eldest son went into medicine and became a general practitioner, the youngest became an accountant, and Philip followed in his father's footsteps, helping to run the newspaper.

Frederick's two daughters married and settled down. The youngest girl lived with her husband and son in a comfortable apartment, quite near to him in Richmond. Susannah, the light of his life, had married a lecturer, who had secured an enviable post at Edinburgh University. It saddened his heart the day she moved north of the border, but he always enjoyed the trips to see her. He particularly remembered the family outing to Loch Lomond, the sparkling waters of the loch, the towering majesty of Ben Lomond, the vivid purple of thousands upon thousands of foxgloves and the perfume of the heather.

Florence was his constant companion through the trials and tribulations of his life, for as well as the good times, Frederick had suffered his fair share of problems like everybody else. The most crashing blow came when his creditors united and took legal action, forcing him into bankruptcy and throwing his life into chaos. Only for the devotion and support of Florence and his children, Frederick doubted if he would live through this crippling ordeal.

One day, in the midst of his gloom, he received the news that he had been left a fair sum of money in a will. An aunt on his mother's side had passed away and, to his great surprise, she had remembered him in a most generous way.

That night, for the first time in months, Frederick was able to sleep soundly in his bed. But after falling asleep something made him jump. He opened his eyes to find that he was still holding his book in his hands. He glanced to the side of his bed and in the bright moonlight he could see the thin column of smoke rising from the candle which he had extinguished only *moments* beforehand.

The above story illustrates how time can play tricks with our minds. Because we associate the passing of time with events, we could be in danger of living in a delusion, a total misrepresentation of the true concept of time.

Because we live in the three dimensional world of gross matter, it is almost impossible for our material brains to deal with events which spring from a non-material world of more than three dimensions. If we could free ourselves from thinking of time in the normal way, subject to the tick of the clock, perhaps we could then make sense of the many accounts of people who have suddenly found themselves cast into what they describe as a timeslip.

Mrs. Sally Vinson of Waltham Abbey in Essex had the most strange experience when she travelled through France some years ago with two friends. They were on their way to Morocco, and not having much money they slept in farmhouses rather than hotels.

They came to a small town in the Garonne Valley not far from Toulouse. They would shortly be crossing the border into Spain, so their first thought was to find a bank or a bureau to change their money into Spanish currency. Sally spotted a policeman, ran up to him and explained in her best broken French what her problem was.

'The policeman seemed to understand what I wanted. He pointed towards a rather quaint looking small hotel and told me to enquire at the reception desk, and they should be able to change the money.

'I waved to my two friends and the three of us started to walk towards the hotel, which was across a square of paving stones. The oddest thing happened as we moved towards the hotel. I felt myself hovering about six inches up in the air. I was stunned at how I did not fall over. I didn't know what on earth was happening. I looked at my two friends and instantly I could see by the startled looks on their faces that they too were experiencing something most strange. They also had the sensation floating.

'It was so sudden and unbelievable that I think we were beyond fear, or perhaps we were reacting directly to fear because all three of us started to laugh. When I think about it now it was probably some sort of nervous reaction, although we were not actually aware of feeling afraid. I suppose if I had been on my own I would have been terrified out of my mind, but because the others were sharing the experience it somehow struck us as being hysterically funny because we just couldn't understand what was happening.

'The odd thing was that all three of us were able to communicate between ourselves in the normal way, so we knew that all of us had the feeling of floating. We were tickled by the fact that we did not need to take steps in order to move, we just seemed to glide forwards. The more this went on the more uncontrollable our laughter became. I could feel tears of mirth running down my cheeks. I remember remarking to one of my friends that if anyone was watching us they would think we were lunatics. Even this simple remark seemed to send us into convulsions of giggles. I think we were imagining how we must look to anyone passing by.

'We reached the hotel and entered. No-one was at the reception desk. We all noticed that the decor was very old-fashioned, but that did not strike us as particularly out of the ordinary because lots of little hotels in France have an old world feel to them.

'We rang the bell on the counter, but no-one came to see what we wanted. By this time we had calmed down slightly, but we still had the sensation of floating. I think we were slowly becoming acclimatized to the condition. After waiting a few moments longer, we decided to have a wander around the hotel to see if we could find anyone who could change our money.

'Just adjacent to the end of the counter was a wide staircase. We walked up the stairs, or should I say floated, and when we got to the top we followed a long corridor which had several windows with coloured glass in them. There was a strange bright light in this corridor, much too bright to have come from the windows. I remember thinking that normally stained glass windows only cast a dim glow, even when strong sunlight shines through them, but this was no ordinary light, as it did not appear to come from any particular direction, and I could not see any shadows, the light just seemed to come from nowhere and everywhere.

'As we moved along the corridor, we could see ahead of us now there was a long landing which went off to the left. At the point where the landing branched off there was a huge mirror, which reached right up to the ceiling. As we approached the mirror, we could see the reflection of our corridor. It looked very long, as if it were going on forever. We kept advancing towards this mirror in a very relaxed state of euphoria. I distinctly remember saying the words "Curiouser and curiouser" because the mirror reminded me of Alice in Wonderland. It was only when I heard the sound of my voice that I seemed to snap out of the malaise with a jerk. I screamed at my two friends, "There's no reflection!" We were almost on top of the mirror, yet there was no reflection of our bodies whatsoever.

'The very next instant our reflections flashed on to the surface of the mirror, just as we were about to smash into it. I don't know how we didn't have a terrible accident. My foot must have only been a fraction away from the glass. It was the most weird thing I've ever seen in my life, the way the three reflections suddenly loomed back at us in that flash. My friends said that they both saw it in exactly the same way.

'By this time all the laughter had gone, and we were all quite afraid. We just stood there for a few moments, very shaken. We all had the same thought uppermost in our minds, what would have happened if I had not spoken out loud and broken the spell, or whatever it was. We wondered if we really would have been able to step right back through that mirror and into some other dimension.

'When we realized that we all now had our feet firmly back on the ground, we decided to forget about changing our money. All we wanted to do was to get out of that place as quickly as possible. We then became aware of the fact that everything was perfectly silent. There were no sounds of any description, apart from our own voices. Somehow it was not a natural quiet, but something more eerie. We looked at each other, then all of us started to run back down the corridor.

'I'm not quite sure exactly what happened at this point, but I think we must have passed the entrance to the top of the staircase leading down to the ground floor. Anyway, we came to a room with wide open double doors. We were absolutely petrified when we looked inside and saw five or six very old ladies sitting inside, all doing embroidery. They were all dressed from head to toe in black and each of them wore a black lace bonnet.

'One of the old ladies saw us, then she beckoned to her companions and they all turned and stared at us. Their faces were white with fear and there was terror in their eyes. Whatever it was about me and my friends seemed to scare the wits out of them. Mind you, we were just as terrified ourselves.

'The three of us took off as fast as we could to try to find the way out of the hotel. Eventually we found a different staircase and got out into the street. We were all in a dreadful state of shock. Needless to say, we moved out of the town as fast as we could. That night we were still afraid and nervous of every building, so we decided to sleep out in the open. We were thankful when we crossed the border into Spain. When I think back to that experience I can't help wondering if we were caught up in a time-warp of some description.'

Mrs. Trenchard of Falmouth in Cornwall had a strange experience when one day she floated out of her body. Completely out of the blue, she found herself in a fairly large room which she had never seen before. She could not understand how she got there and had no recollection of a journey.

'There were bare boards on the floor and in the middle of the room there was a smallish rug, rather faded. There was furniture around the sides of the room, rather indistinct, the middle of the room being bare. I looked down at my feet and I was amazed to find myself suddenly wearing roller skates. "This is crazy," I thought to myself, "I don't wear roller skates. I never even wore them as a child, how ridiculous!" However, I then found myself starting to skate up and down the boards and rug.

'My mind was very alert. I said to myself that I will always remember this as everything seemed so real and vivid. The lightness of my body gave me such a lovely feeling, and I smiled as I realized that my bad foot, which had always given me much trouble, was now at perfect ease, despite the fact that I was skating up and down.

'I was intrigued to find that the rug in the middle of the floor did not hamper the skating and in fact there did not seem to be any friction at all, as the skates just glided over the floorboards and rug. I skated backwards and forwards several times, thoroughly enjoying myself, thinking how fantastic it was.

'I have to explain something before I come to the next part of the story; my mother, who was a good pianist, had a Bechstein grand piano. When she grew old and could no longer see well enough to play, the piano was sold to a neighbour who was an acquaintance of mine, but I had never been inside her bungalow.

'From the roadway, this woman's place looked so small that one would have thought that there would be no room for a grand piano inside. Apparently she had a large basement which I did not know existed, since it was below the level of the road.

'Shortly after I had experienced the skating, I was walking past this woman's bungalow, and she happened to be standing at her front door. She called out to me and said, "Thelma, do come in and see your mother's piano. We've had it restored. We spent £80 on it and it looks like new."

'I went in and was shown down to the basement. Immediately my blood ran cold as I recognized the floorboards and the faded rug. It gave me quite a shock. I said,

"What a lovely big room you have." "Yes," she said, "When my grandchildren were small we used to clear the furniture to the side and they used to skate in here."

A lady from Stevenage had a dream that she was alone in a very big rambling house. She knew that she was waiting to let the gas man in to read the meter. At the time she had the dream she was single, but in this dream she was engaged to a young dark-haired man. In reality she knew no such person.

About ten years later, she met a man at a party and became quite attracted to him. There was something vaguely familiar about him, but she could not quite pinpoint exactly what it was or where she might have seen him. They went out together for a few months and soon realized that they had fallen in love. They became engaged and they decided to look for a small flat in Margate on the south coast of Kent, as his family lived down there, although at the time they both lived in London.

On the first flat-hunting session in Margate, they naturally arranged to visit the man's parents as she had not yet been introduced to the family. They were invited to dinner, but when they got to the house they found a note on the narrow window ledge and a key. The note was from the man's mother, informing him that she would be back later, but would he let himself in. Also, would he mind showing the gas man where the meter was, as she had received a card from the gas board, informing her that someone would be calling to check the meter that day.

As soon as she stepped into the house, everything came flooding back to her. It was the exact same house of which she had dreamt all those years before. A further thought then struck her. She turned and looked at her fiancé's face.

Yes! It was the same man! Now everything clicked into place. That's why she felt that there had been something familiar about him on their first meeting.

'I was quite taken aback when I realized that the details were so exact, right down to the business about letting in the gas man. In my dream I never saw the gas man arrive as I woke up before that happened, but I've often wondered if it would have been the same man who, just a few minutes later, knocked on the door and came in to check the meter.

'I truly believe that I was meant to meet my fiance. We have since married and are very happy. We both believe that there must be something in the old saying that marriages are made in Heaven, at least we're sure ours was.'

Some years ago, when she lived in central London, Mary Harrison, the co-author of this book, had a strange dream which took her back in time to the days of Bonnie Prince Charlie and the Battle of Culloden.

'I was in a small boat with Peter and an elderly white haired man whom I'd never seen before. He was dressed in what could only be described as a long navy overall, which was wrapped around him and secured by a belt or cord around the waist. The water was quite shallow and, as the tiny boat drifted towards the side bank, we all got out. There were two tall, thin evergreen trees by the bank and as I stepped out of the boat, to the right, there stood a big mansion house, with a flight of steps leading up to a large front door.

'We all started walking towards the house. Nothing was said at this point. We walked up the stairs and the man opened the door. We entered the house, which was completely unknown to me. I remember thinking how elegant and grand it looked. We walked across a large hall area, and proceeded up a flight of steps. After a few steps my attention became attracted by the bannister. Because the staircase was wide, I somehow or another expected it to be of polished wood. I was quite surprised to see that the handrail was, in fact, covered with what I took to be red and white brocade material. I stopped and looked over at this as it made such a strange impression upon me, making me curious to find out why there should be such an unusual covering over the broad handrail.

'At that point, the elderly man who, with Peter, had been walking a few steps ahead of me up the staircase, came back down to where I was standing. He too looked across at the bannister and said, "You are interested in this, let me show you." With that he took my arm and led me over to inspect the handrail. To my horror, as I moved nearer, I realized that what I thought was a red and white pattern was actually blood stains. When I looked closely I could see that the white part was made up of lots and lots of bandages. It was as if masses of blood-stained bandages had been wrapped around and around the length of the handrail.

'The man could see that I was shocked. He said, "These are the bandages from the Battle of Culloden. If you look closely, you will see the names of the people who were killed, and alongside their names it states the type of weapon which killed them." I studied the material, and I could distinctly see lots of names, written in what looked like faded navy blue ink. The entries appeared on the white section of the cloth, but always alongside a bloodstain. I could not make out what was written, but there were about three or four lines of writing for each different name.

'I remember the overwhelming feeling of sorrow that

engulfed me at that moment. I looked up and down the bannister at the dozens and dozens of names. In that one instant I felt the grief of all those families and the pain surrounding each of those faded names.

'The man then pulled me away from the side of the staircase, saying, "Don't look at it too much, we've got to go now." He guided me up the stairs to a landing from which the stairway branched out at either side close to each wall, turning back in the opposite direction, leading up to the next floor. Along this landing against the far wall there was a row of what looked like old fashioned tailor's dummies. Each one was dressed in a different tartan, representing the different clans which fought in the Battle of Culloden. I turned to the left and by the far wall there was an oak panelled door. I stretched out my hand to open this door, but I never found out what was on the other side because at that point I woke up.

'The dream was so clear that I, of course, related it to Peter there and then. After that there came a stream of coincidences. A few days later I opened a book which I had just got out from the Marylebone Library entitled *The Mask of Time, The Mystery Factor in Timeslip, Precognition and Hindsight*, by Joan Forman (Corgi). I was casually looking down the acknowledgements page, when I suddenly spotted "The Culloden Trust". I was immediately interested to see what this was about. It led me to a particular story in that book which told of how a woman from East Anglia had travelled to Scotland on a coach tour. They reached the battlefield of Culloden on a warm, sunny August afternoon. The crowd got out of the coach and started to eat their sandwiches.

'Suddenly, the sky clouded over and became grey, damp

and misty. The woman could not see any of her companions, but instead she was faced with a solitary hawthorn tree. There were no leaves on the tree but, blowing in the breeze, draped from the branches, she could see long, white, blood-stained bandages. She stared hard at this peculiar sight, then she heard a voice telling her, "These are the bandages from the Battle of Culloden."

'The next instant the tree and the bandages disappeared and the woman could hear the chatter of her friends and one more she felt the warming rays of the sun!'

Mary was struck by this, especially as the words which the woman heard were identical to those which the old man said to her in her dream.

'I had never been to Culloden, not had I any particular link with that part of Scotland. I remembered having been told about the battle at school, and I do admit that in the history lessons there was something about Culloden which always upset me more than any other event. In fact, I remember, as a little girl, trying to hide my face with my hands when the teacher spoke to us about the massacre, so that no-one would see that I was crying. But all of that was years ago, and I had not even given it a thought since then.

'The next thing that happened was a small package was delivered by post. I almost fainted when I opened it to find a brochure with a picture of a huge mansion house on the front and the words "Culloden House". This was within a week of my dream. Because we had been thinking of buying an hotel, we had approached a few agents and by a strange turn of fate, Culloden House, which unbeknown to me had been converted into an hotel, was on the market.

'I'd never seen Culloden House, or even a photograph of it, up to that point. I stared at the mansion, and it looked exactly like the house I'd seen in my dream when I'd stepped out of the boat. I was sure in my mind that it must be the same house, with the flight of stone steps leading up to the front door.

'I opened up the brochure and there were a few small photographs inside which did not really convey much to me.

'Eventually, some time later, I telephoned Culloden House, as I could not get the dream out of my head. By this time, it had been bought by an hotelier. I was somewhat apprehensive when I first spoke to the proprietor on the phone, as I was not at all sure what I was going to say, or what his reaction would be.

'After the initial niceties, I explained that although it was probably going to sound a bit daft, I just wanted to verify what the interior of the house looked like. I told him about the lake and the trees, the outside of the house and the staircase, also how it branched off into two other side flights of stairs, going up by the side walls. He listened patiently and did not laugh. At that point I did not mention anything about the bandages, I simply wished to find out the layout of the house.

'He confirmed that there had been a shallow lake at the front of the house and, in fact, the two tall trees were still there. He told me that the large hallway was correct, also the elaborate staircase, but there the similarity ended because the stairs did not branch out and go up by the side of each wall, as I explained had happened in the dream.

'I thanked him for his information and remarked that it must be a weird coincidence. However, two nights later, I received a telephone call from Culloden House. The owner had been so intrigued by my query that he had gone to his local planning department, and had been allowed to see the plans for when the original old house had been extended.

'"You were right," he told me excitedly. "The original stairs did branch out exactly as you described, but when they extended the property, they partitioned one of the staircases off. Also, the door on the landing did exist."

'It was with mixed feelings that I received this news. It was not exactly a surprise as I seemed to "know" inwardly that these stairs did exist at some time in the past in precisely the same way as I saw them.'

chapter eleven

THE DECISION

In almost any account of out-of-the-body travel, the person reports that at some point they are faced with a decision. To many, this was the most important decision of their lives, in fact they feel it was a definite choice between life and death.

Mrs. Radnell of Nottingham was so concerned about her children that she made the conscious decision to try to get back into her body. She says, 'In the summer of 1983 I fell asleep whilst lying on my side on the settee; I had my arms folded at the time. Having slept normally for some time I awoke and found I was drifting into one of my "sleep paralysis" states. I tried not to panic, and thought if I could just move an arm, I would be O.K. But, unfortunately, I had my arms folded and this made it doubly difficult. Just when I thought my arms were unfolding, I found instead that I sort of "peeled" out of my body. The next moment I was standing by the gas fire, which was directly in front of the settee. To describe the terror and panic I felt is impossible; it is something I will never forget.

'I knew my body was back on the settee, but I just didn't dare look. I felt very distressed because I realized that the children would find the body on the settee, would think it was "me" and this would break their hearts. There would be no way of communicating to them, or anyone else, that I was perfectly O.K. I really believed I was dying on the settee, and I was panic stricken. Just as I was thinking, "Oh, no I'm dying", the thought came into my mind, "No, not dying, out of the body," but it was as if another mind had locked into mine and so closely was it overlapping, that grammatical sentences were not necessary. However, I saw no-one nor had I any mystical experience.

'What I did notice was that I could think and feel things at an incredibly fast speed, so that whilst I was wondering who I might see, I could also think, "What do I look like?" "What is the time?" etc. I did notice that I had no concept of time, and had no idea of where the children were. Also, I felt very flat and flimsy and sort of "whole" – by this I mean that I felt I could form arms and legs if I wanted to, because I considered the idea of lifting an "arm" to see what it looked like, but I chickened out!

'I think the biggest impact the experience had on me was to realize that I was exactly the same person as I am in the body, and this pleased and reassured me. I even noticed I could swear if I wanted to (something I do far too much of).

'Another thing I noticed was that I felt vulnerable and unprotected without my "shell" and soon wanted to be back "inside". I remember praying something like, "Oh God, (expletive) I don't want this," and the second I thought this I began travelling backwards towards my physical body. I could feel a tremendous sucking sensation in the region of my "ethereal" cheeks and I travelled back very quickly. In front of me, but not part of me, was a whirling circular shaped object, made of a sort of vapour (I could see the bookcases through it). Soon I was back in the body, jolted upright with a start and feeling very shaken.

'I told my husband what had happened but, like most people, he was sceptical and said I had dreamt it. But to me it was very, very real. I am willing to tell anyone if it can bring comfort to those who think they have "lost" their loved ones, in order to reassure them that we do survive physical death.'

A new-born baby was the incentive for Mrs. Bartlett of Birmingham to return. She remembers floating just below the ceiling in the corner of the room, looking down on the scene below, where medical staff were attending to her physical body. 'I was feeling warm and peaceful, and could see the bright sunlight which attracted me forward. There were soft country sounds and I felt I must be on holiday. I watched the figure on the bed with all the people around her. I then looked down beneath me at the tiny baby in the cot. I felt as if I'd shouted out, "Why that's me down there. I can't leave that baby there – she's mine. I must get back!" The sun faded away and it all went black. Someone was calling my name. When I awoke, it was night, and no-one was there but my sister-in-law, holding a cup to my mouth.

'I was told afterwards that the doctors had worked on me for over two hours and did not expect me to survive.'

Chris Broad of Newcastle has built up an understandable apprehension regarding the medical profession. He has had two out-of-the-body experiences, but he is very glad he made the decision to come back both times.

'The first occasion I was about twelve years old when I was knocked off my pedal cycle by a doctor in a car. I clearly recall being about telegraph pole height and seeing the crowd. At first I did not notice it was me down there but I recognized my cycle and when I saw myself I could not be sure what to do – go up or come down. I was so happy. Then I thought of my family, mother, father, brother, sister, and how upset they would be, so down I came, into my body. It was like putting on a boiler suit! Honestly, I can still feel the sensation of climbing into it. Then, in a flash I was back and on the ground, with all these faces looking down at me, so I got up amid gasps and staggered to my cycle.

'The second occasion was similar. I was thirty-six when I was knocked off my motor-cycle – again by a doctor in a car! Then I thought of my wife and four young children. I was happy up there but I knew I had to get back for their sakes. They needed me and I wanted to see them grow up. So, down I came. Again it was like putting on a boiler suit. I could see the crowd from above and two damaged cars, my crushed motor-cycle and myself in black motor-cycle clothing on the road. I found it amusing when I went down. I thought I will surprise the crowd!

'Both times though, it was a very pleasant and wonderful feeling. I was tempted to go higher because I felt so free and happy – the hurt came when I returned! If I do have another out-of-the-body experience I think I will go higher out of curiosity.

'I am very happy with my life and pleased that I came back. I am trying to avoid any doctors driving cars!'

It was the love of her husband which was the trigger which enabled Mrs. Cumberledge (a first cousin of Enid Blyton) of Eastbourne in Sussex to return. 'One lovely summer's day I had just come home from my work in a dress shop. It was my half-day and I was feeling fed up. I went up to bed and thought, "I wish I could go to sleep and not wake up." Well, I woke up out of my body. I checked the time by the clock at the side of the bed – nearly 3.45 p.m. I was not frightened or alarmed, but I was concerned, knowing what my thoughts had been. Now I thought while checking the time, "I'm dead!" I thought of what a shock it would be for my husband who would be home around 5.20 p.m. "Well," I thought, "I've got from 3.45 to 5.20 to work out how I'm going to get back." Then I looked at myself lying in bed and thought, "I must get back." Then, back I was. I checked the clock to find that only a few seconds had passed.'

The conviction that she was choking frightened a lady from Toddington, Bedfordshire, back down into her body. 'I floated out of my body and right out through the open window. It was light and I remember quite distinctly that I was "floating" in a sitting or curled up position (perhaps the embryonic position). There were long, thin gardens all divided by tall hedges on either side. I floated up the gardens, having to rise slightly over each hedge. I remember wondering if I put my legs out straight if they would scrape on the hedges – but I never tried it.

'I'd got about ten houses up when I had the most urgent, choking, cold feeling that I had to get back. I felt like I'd come out in a cold sweat. I sped back, bouncing over the fences, rushed through the windows, and no hanging about, shot over to my sleeping body, when I instantly woke up, puffed, heart beating fast – I was quite convinced that if I'd not got there in time, my body would have been dead. It was an incredible sense of relief I'd made it. I didn't want to be shut out."

In his book *Reach for the Sky* (Collins, hardback, 1954; Fontana, paperback, 1969), Paul Brickhill relates how the famous Second World War air ace Group Captain Douglas Bader was faced with a similar decision. He had an odd experience while in hospital after losing his legs in a flying accident. It did not occur to him that he had been dying until after he had made his decision.

Later the young man woke and the pain had gone. He could not feel his body at all, but for some reason his mind was perfectly clear. He lay still, eyes open and head raised on a pillow, looking straight out

118

through the top of the window at a patch of clear blue sky, and into his mind crept a peaceful thought: 'This is pleasant. I've only got to shut my eyes now and lean back and everything's all right.' Warm peace was stealing over him, his eyes closing and his head seeming to sink into the pillow. It did not occur to him that he was dying; only that he was letting go, drifting down and wanting to. In a dreamy haze the mind was shrinking into a soft, deep pinpoint.

Through the slightly open door of the room a woman's disembodied voice slid into the receding clarity: 'Sssh! Don't make so much noise. There's a boy dying in there.'

The words quivered in him like a little electric shock that froze the drifting dream and sparked a sharp thought: 'So that's it. Hell, am I!' Feeling began flickering out through his body like ripples from a pebble tossed in a pool. He stopped letting go and the mind was clearing; the body did not move but the brain began gripping thought and reality. It was the challenge that stirred him...

As he lay thinking, quite clear-headed, the pain came back to his leg. Somehow he did not mind this time; it was almost satisfying because he felt he was normal again and had slipped away from the ethereal spirit that had been floating him to Limbo. Another thought came: 'I mustn't let that happen again. Apparently it wasn't as good as it felt.'

Some instinct told him that he had been dying in that moment. (Ever since then he has been convinced of it, and from that moment has never been frightened of dying. Later this was to have a vital effect on his life).

One of the most peculiar stories of decision making comes from a lady in Nottingham, who reports a weird administration problem in the afterworld.

'I was ill in hospital, just lying in bed, thinking of nothing in particular when I felt a "swoosh" and, to my amazement, I found myself hovering in mid-air above my hospital bed. I felt quite fine apart from being utterly puzzled at the fact that I could see myself lying in bed. I just couldn't understand what was happening to me. The next thing I knew, I was gently moving along the corridor outside the hospital ward. This corridor somehow or other turned into a narrow passage of extremely bright light. I began to feel uneasy at this stage, because I had lost sight of my physical body, and I had an overpowering feeling that I shouldn't really be in this passageway, although at that stage I was unable to stop myself moving forward.

'The end of the tunnel came into view in the form of an archway. I could not see anyone but I sensed that someone was standing there.

'I distinctly heard a woman's voice saying, "Oh, just a moment, we only wanted two. We've got one already and anyway it's not time for you at the moment." Again the woman's voice stated, "We've got one already!" Then the voice added in a most apologetic tone, "Would you mind going back?"

'As soon as I heard her say that, I thought about the hospital ward. I started to feel worried about what the sister would say to me for being away so long. I began to wonder what I would tell them, and then I convinced myself that I was in for a right telling-off for wandering away like that. I don't remember anything at all about what happened next, except waking up in my bed in the early hours of the morning. I could hear a man's voice out in the corridor. He sounded most distressed as he explained to the nurse that he had received an urgent call to come into the hospital because his mother had died.

'I've often wondered to myself if that poor man's mother was the "other" person that the woman at the arch awaited. Somehow they got me instead, but sent me packing as it were!

'Since that experience, I have no fear of death whatsoever, because I've seen what lies ahead and it is truly beautiful.'

chapter twelve

THE SILVER CORD

Many poems and songs refer to the Silver Cord, or the Golden Thread or the Cord of Light. Different names have been given to this part of ethereal matter which connects the astral body, which contains the soul, to the physical body.

In most reports of out-of-body travel, people are so disorientated by the different conditions into which they have been hurled that they do not notice anything connecting them with their physical bodies which they can see, either lying on a bed, walking or setting on a chair, etc. It takes some moments for consciousness to become accustomed to the change. The first, and most impressive, perception which the wandering spirit experiences is the feeling of weightlessness. After living for years and years in the heavy material world of gross matter, suddenly the spirit escapes from the restraints of gravity. The result of this is the almost unbelievable feeling that the entire being is as light as a feather, just floating effortlessly.

Most people remember this as a delightful experience, comprised of a strange mixture of exhilaration and peace. The material body is without senses at this point, all the perception and feeling being contained in the released spirit body.

As you can imagine, this sudden change in vibrations, coupled with having to adapt to totally different laws of creation, overpowers the spirit so much that it is not altogether surprising that some factors of this new experience may be overlooked by the awe-struck spirit consciousness.

121

Nevertheless, some people have observed the connecting cord between their hovering spirit bodies and their physical shells.

A lady of Northampton describes what happened to her husband. 'One night when we were in bed, I woke up. He was holding on to me so tightly that I could hardly breathe. When I asked him what was the matter, he said that he had been "frightened that he couldn't get back". I asked him what on earth he was talking about, then added, "It must have been a dream." He was adamant that it had not been a dream and that he had left his body and was floating around the room in mid-air. He told me that he could see himself but that he was attached to his solid body by a fine thread. He was very afraid.

'He could see the thin thread coming from the part of him that was floating, going towards and connecting with his physical body lying beside me on the bed. He was terrified that the thread might somehow get broken and he was convinced that if that happened then he would never get back into his body. He was sure that he would be dead to this world.

'To be honest, I have to admit that it all sounds totally ridiculous, doesn't it? I've not spoken about it to anyone because they would probably think we were both barmy.'

A somewhat similar story comes from Janet White of Southampton. She remembers that when her daughter was being born, she drifted out of her body and, from high up in the corner of the room, she found herself looking down on the nurses in the delivery room. 'It was a wonderful, strange feeling. I seemed to have a fine thread holding me to my

122

body. I remember being fascinated by this thread, and as I moved, or should I say floated, the thread seemed to stretch with me. It must have been made of an elastic-type material, which could stretch as far as I cared to make it. When I floated down nearer to my body, the thread just shortened accordingly. It was the strangest thing I ever saw in my life. I had all my reasoning powers with me up there and as I looked down upon the scene below, I was perfectly aware of the fact that I was in the process of giving birth. Although I could comprehend this, I did not, for some reason, feel particularly affected. The overpowering thought that seemed to take over my mind completely was the fact that all the horrible pain had gone. I had been lying on that delivery bed in unbearable agony just a few seconds ago, and now look at me. No pain or discomfort whatsoever. In fact, it was the exact opposite, I'd never felt better or more happy in my life.

'I then felt myself being drawn slowly back down towards the bed. As I hovered just a few feet above, I seemed to be able to pass right through the bodies of three nurses who were attending to me. I remember feeling most apologetic for having "bumped into them", and I was expecting them to be a bit annoyed but, to my surprise, they did not react in any way. They completely ignored me as if I didn't exist, and they didn't seem to feel a thing when I was knocking into them on my way back down to my body.

'I could see one of the nurses slapping my face. I was taken aback by this and wondered why she should do such a thing. Then, as if far away in the distance, I heard the words "Come on, come on, it's all over now, come on." The words got louder in my ears and made me open my eyes. I knew that I was now back in my physical body. The nurse was still slapping my face. It was then I heard the cries of a baby. "It's a lovely little girl" the nurse told me, and I fully realized that my baby had just been born.

'A great gush of love washed over me and I couldn't wait to hold my baby. I stretched out for her and the tiny little bundle was placed in my arms. As I looked adoringly down at the little pink face and the mop of golden hair, which was still matted with blood, I remember wondering how I could have felt so indifferently towards her whilst I was out of my body. Maybe it was because at that point I had not actually seen her. All I could do was hug her and look at her in wonderment. At that moment I truly felt that she was worth all the pain and suffering I had just gone through, and I would not have changed it for the world.'

Yet another version of how the cord has been witnessed comes from a lady who had a dream that she awoke in what she thought was a morgue.

'I was lying on a marble slab, but I felt completely fit and well, and I could not understand why I should be there. I'd seen such places in films and I remember thinking that only dead people are brought to places like this. I grew more and more uneasy as my mind started to run riot, and I got frightened in case I should be put in a freezer or sent to a crematorium. I started to call out, but there was no sign of anyone. I then started to panic, calling out as loud as I could, "I'm not dead, I'm not dead." I sat up on the slab and got the shock of my life when I spotted just further along that there was another marble slab and another version of me. It was like looking at a twin, but I never had a twin. I sat up as much as I could to have a better look. I noticed that the other me was quite ashen looking and lay silent and still.

'By this time I was in a state of complete confusion. I genuinely thought that the other "me" must really be dead. I called over to the other body, "Merle, are you all right?" It was an odd feeling, because I knew that I was talking to myself, but it became more and more disturbing because the other Merle did not seem to hear me calling and made no response whatsoever.

'In the back of my mind I had a recollection of the old saying that when people start to talk to themseles, that is the first sign of madness. I thought about this and wondered to myself whether or not I really might be going mad. But then I calmed down a bit when I considered that I was still able to think in a clear rational way, surely mad people couldn't do this.

'What I could not come to grips with was the fact that the thinking me, the real me, felt quite natural and alive. What was disrupting my logical mind was this other "me".

'I decided that the only way I would ever find out what was going on would be to take a closer look. I eased myself off the marble slab. This was not difficult to do because I just seemed to glide off with hardly any effort. I stood upright but I don't remember feeling my feet touch the floor. I was so light that I was literally standing on air, ridiculous as this may seem.

'As soon as I stood upright I noticed a long silver cord which connected me with my other body. I don't know how I never spotted it before. Perhaps it was because it appeared to come out of me in the same way as an umbilical cord attaches a baby to its mother.

'I then became aware of the presence of other people in this morgue, although I could not actually see them. I was so concerned about the Merle who was still stretched out motionless on the other slab, so I asked the people who I felt were present, "Is she all right?" They answered me, "Yes, she is all right."

'The answer came as a great relief to me, so I then proceeded to float above the marble slab. I experienced a tremendous uplifting feeling of well-being and I noticed that whenever I chose to move, I did not have to make any effort at all. It sounds quite incredible, but I only had to think of moving to any particular area and off I would float. It was as simple as that.

'The other thing that I found bewildering was that wherever I floated, the cord which connected me with my other body seemed to lengthen itself. It felt as if I could go as far as I like and this cord would still travel with me, stretching as far as it needed to stretch to allow me to move freely to where I wanted to go.

'The reverse also was true. When I moved nearer to the marble slab where my other body lay, the cord automatically reduced its length so that there was not any extra cord lying around which was not required.

'It reminded me of when I used to wind up my wool into balls for knitting. I had a little playful kitten at the time, and it delighted in unravelling the wool from the nearly made up balls. The only difference was that when my kitten drew out long stretches of wool, it would all lie in a jumbled up heap on the floor until I wound it all up again, whereas with this silver cord, it just fed itself back into my body, so that only what was required would be left out.

'I have never felt so much at peace with the world as when I had that dream, if it was only a dream. Sometimes, I wonder!'

A Newtownabbey lady was working as a weaver in a factory. 'It was very noisy, with twelve looms in three rows of four. One of the looms stopped, indicating a broken thread, so I leaned over to tie the thread in. I felt the strange sensation of drifting out of my body and then I floated up to the rafters.

'There was a wisp of silvery smoke between me and my body. I seemed to be travelling towards a light. In my head something said, "Not yet." I came back into my body with such a bang that I hurt by chest. Whilst I was up in the rafters I could not hear the looms. I remember looking around but no-one seemed to notice anything strange. There were no bruises afterwards, and I felt fine, but how I got up to these rafters still baffles me.'

The only experience the authors have had regarding the cord is when Mary had yet another one of her strange dreams.

'I found myself standing in a pleasant place which I did not recognize, but where I felt somehow or another at home. I could hear sounds of laughter and the general noises of people enjoying themselves.

'I was suddenly in the midst of my dead mother, father and aunt. They had bright, shining faces, all looked extremely happy and young. They all gave me the most tremendous welcome as if they were delighted to see me, but there was something of a novel feel to it all. I got the definite feeling that they knew something that I didn't. Being my usual inquisitive self, I asked them why they were all laughing in such a way. I might add that it was not in any way a jeering laughter, but more the type of laugh which one gives when one is faced with a sudden, but pleasant surprise. I suppose it can be compared to the laugh at the end of a joke which has a benevolent twist to the punch-line.

'Anyway, I knew perfectly well that something was taking place which I did not fully understand. It was so natural to be in the company of these beloved people that I was completely at ease, with no real reason to question anything except for the expression on my father's face. He always loved a joke and I recognized the impish twinkle in his eyes.

' "Come on, what are you up to?" I asked him. This question set him off into roars of laughter. My mother and aunt just laughed along with him, then I remember my mother giving my father a kind of familiar warning look, as if to say, "Don't tease her!"

'At that moment something drew my attention to the fact that something was shining behind me. I looked around quickly and saw what looked like a rope of luminous light somehow attached to me.

' "What's that?" I asked them. They stopped laughing and told me, "It's all right." I started to fidget and then tried to grasp this rope to free myself of it. At this point my mother became most alarmed and told me: "Stop pulling it. You need it. Everything is all right." My father put his hand out to stop me from trying to back away from the rope. My mother's words were solemn as she said, "She'll have to go back now!"

'As soon as she said these words I felt an enormous pull from behind as if I had been swooshed right off my feet and into the air. This happened so quickly that I did not even have time to say "Good-bye" to them as I was hurled away without warning.

'I've often thought about what might have happened if

I'd managed to free myself of that cord. I have the strong feeling that although my parents were thrilled to see me again they were, as usual, protecting me by sending me back to my life on this earth, to Peter and the children.'

chapter thirteen

COINCIDENCE

Have you ever tried to explain a coincidence? It is one of the most difficult tasks to undertake. Maybe there is no explanation which we can grasp with our material conscious brains, but nevertheless there must be an explanation.

It may be that because the experiences cover such a wide range, the explanation lies in more than one source. For example, some experiences may be the result of telepathy, others the manifestation of true extra-sensory perception, some may be down to pure chance, and others may be linked into our fate.

Instances of *déjà vu* have been experienced by most of us, whereby you may enter a room for the first time and immediately you have the strong feeling that you have been there before, in exactly the same circumstances with exactly the same people. Most people will go as far as to state that because the feeling of having done it all before was so unmistakable, they were able to foretell what was going to be said next, and by whom. These feelings do not seem to last for very long, and in all cases, it is impossible to recall when the previous 'visitation' to that particular room occurred.

There are various theories on *déjà vu*. It is thought that one eye takes in information and relays this to the brain slightly faster than the other eye. By the time the comparatively sluggish eye surveys the scene and makes a mental note of it, the work of processing the data has already been completed by the brain on the instructions sent to it by the eye which first viewed the scene. From this, therefore, follows the familiar feeling of having seen it all before. In this case it is not that you have experienced the scene twice, simply that the brain has been given the same message twice, once by each eye.

In some cases this could well be an explanation; however, the argument is eliminated when we hear of cases where people are walking up a street for the first time, but the surroundings are so familiar that they feel they have been there before. They even know what is going to be round the next corner. Now, because human eyes can't see round corners, there must be other factors at play in these cases. Could it be that during these flashes, the unsuspecting people have a flash of intuition whereby their ethereal bodies have been able to view the entire scene from a point above, this information has then been conveyed to the sub-conscious mind, which in turn transfers it to the conscious mind? It is a simple explanation and perfectly logical.

Mrs. Elizabeth Smith from Amersham in Buckinghamshire still cannot explain a coincidence which took place a few years ago, when she was sitting under the dryer at the local hairdresser's, leafing through some magazines and casually exchanging a few words with a woman sitting next to her, who was also having her hair dried. She had never seen this woman before in her life.

As Elizabeth turned the pages of the magazine she saw a photograph of a luxurious bathroom which she and the other woman admired.

'I then said that the grandest bathroom that I had ever encountered had been in an old house in Scotland, and not only were the bathroom fittings of an Edwardian grandeur, but there were tanks of fish in the room. I went on to tell the woman next to me that the house was now owned by my sister-in-law and her husband who is the factor (or estate manager) of a large estate in the north.

'My new-found friend stated that she too had known such a bathroom, and how spendid that one also had been. I explained where "my" house was, near Forres in Morayshire, and she said incredulously that it was precisely the same house about which she had been talking.

'It turned out that she had lived in that house during the war, when the house had been made available to accommodate war service families. She had lived in one of the smaller rooms at the back of the house.

'I don't know what the odds are on such a coincidence might be, extremely high, no doubt. In a sense, however, we both seemed to be approaching the subject by different paths in a logical way towards the incredible dénouement.' Mrs. Smith is a member of the Chesham Bois Women's Institute, but none of the other ladies at her branch can offer her an explanation.

Mr. Chris Smith of Long Eaton, Nottingham, remembers something which happened to him when he was serving with the Military Police, stationed at Edinburgh Castle. His room-mate, also serving with the Military Police, was a local man called Jock Cunningham. 'We had only been sharing the same room for a couple of weeks, but we got on fine and on our time off we used to walk down the Royal Mile to a little pub where we used to have a few drinks and a laugh with some of the locals.

'One night we got acquainted with two girls. We all seemed to spark off great together, so after a few drinks the girl I was with invited us back to her house somewhere on the outskirts of Edinburgh. The four of us got one of those plum coloured corporation buses, and ended up somewhere at the back of beyond.

'After a couple of hours at the house, I could see that Jock was getting on well with his girl, but my girl got drunk and we had a trivial argument. I can't even remember what caused it now. Anyway, I was so cheesed off that I got up and left the house, not knowing from Adam where I was. It was the middle of the night and there was nobody outside in the street at all.

'I just walked and walked, trying to find a main road. At last I came to road signs pointing to Edinburgh, so I started walking along that road. For the first time in my life I thought I'd better try to hitch a lift or I could be walking all night. It was pouring rain at the time, which didn't help matters, and there was little or no traffic on the road.

'Eventually, a white Mercedes, left-hand drive, pulled up and the driver invited me to have a lift. He said that he never ever gives people lifts, but something made him pull up when he saw me. There was no particular reason, he added.

'He asked me where I was going, so I told him "The City Centre." He asked, "Whereabouts?" I told him that I had to get back to Edinburgh Castle. He then said, "Oh, you must be in the Army, what unit?" I replied, "Actually, it's the Military Police." He perked up when I said this and told me, "My son is stationed up there in the Military Police. You might know him, his name is Jock Cunningham."

'I could hardly believe my ears. When I think back on it, I keep pondering on how it could have happened, is this a true coincidence? It is the only time in my life I had ever tried to hitch a lift, Mr. Cunningham did not normally give lifts to people, and Edinburgh is a big city.'

133

A puzzling, but sad, story comes from a man in Luton. 'One Saturday in June I had closed my office and had decided to do some overtime to catch up with the filing and other paperwork. The time was approximately 1.15 p.m. Suddenly, for no reason at all, I fell off my chair. After I got over the initial surprise, I picked myself up off the floor and, of course, the first thing I did was to examine my chair. Everything was intact and I could not see how I had fallen. It was as if some force had knocked me right off the chair. I did not hurt myself unduly, apart from a bruise on the base of the spine, so it was not long before I was back at my desk, working through my papers.

'About half-an-hour later I received a telephone call from my niece who had been visiting us. She sounded petrified on the phone as she asked me to come home immediately. 'What's happened?' I asked. I was told that my little daughter, Sharon, had had a terrible accident, having fallen out of a window, and had been rushed to hospital. I ran from my office in a state of shock, and drove straight to the hospital. As soon as I saw my wife's tragic face I knew the dreadful truth, Sharon was dead. She had died in the ambulance on the way to the hospital. I was completely numb. The days and weeks which followed were like a living nightmare.

'It was a long time before I could bring myself to talk about my daughter, but one night while I was just sitting talking to my wife, something made me ask what time Sharon had fallen. My wife told me that it was exactly 1.15 p.m. because she was just about to serve lunch and she had looked at the clock just as she heard the scream.

'A cold shiver ran through me when I realized that it was precisely at 1.15 p.m. on that same day that I had unaccountably fallen off the chair in my office.

'Several months later on the first anniversary of Sharon's death, my wife and I were sitting quietly at home watching the television and feeling rather low (not unnaturally) when there was an almighty crash, followed by the sound of breaking glass. Sharon's photograph had fallen off the wall. Nobody had been anywhere near the photograph. It was most eerie. To this day I have never been able to understand it.

'We moved house shortly after that because there were too many painful memories there. Since moving nothing out of the ordinary has happened, but I've often thought of what could have caused these events to happen. Could it have been an attempt by my daughter to contact us?'

A gentleman from Wellingborough, Northamptonshire, was serving in the R.A.F. in the Second World War, when he was captured in the Far East. He and a group of fellow prisoners were being transported around the Spice Islands in a ramshackle wooden boat by their Japanese captors to form working parties on the myriad of small islands.

A field gun, with no elevation, was mounted on the bow of the vessel. 'Suddenly we saw something silver, glinting as it flew out of the sun. It was a four-engined aircraft. We knew it was an Allied plane because the Japanese didn't have any four engined planes.

'The Japanese sergeant, who was in charge, ordered the prisoners to wave at the rapidly-approaching aircraft, to show that we were not hostile. Now, this was in September 1944 and we had been prisoners since February 1942. We were clad only in a few rags, we were greatly emaciated and very deeply tanned. We must have appeared very strange to the Allied plane as we waved and cheered.

'The aircraft circled the wooden boat lower and lower,

trying to decide whether we were hostile. In the end, the Japanese gunner lost his nerve and fired the field gun. Of course, he had no hope of hitting the plane because the gun had no elevation.

'The plane flew away, turned and flew back, very low, at great speed, with cannons firing. The result was that the boat disintegrated completely, killing some eight Japanese and twenty prisoners. The survivors were thrown into the shark-infested waters of the Banda Sea, and had to swim for the shore of the nearest island.

'We remained on the island for a few days until a passing Japanese boat picked us up.

'Some years later, I attended a F.E.P.O.W. reunion, and was talking with an old friend of this incident. He told me that he had been drinking in a pub with some friends in Leytonstone, London. They were sitting at a table near to some men who were playing darts. My friend was relating this story, when one of the darts players visibly paled, and came over to their table. He asked if the plane had destroyed the boat near to New Guinea in September 1944. My pal replied that it had, and that he would like to meet the bastard responsible. The darts player slumped into a chair, saying, "Well, mate, you just have! I was the navigator on that flight." He explained that the pilot had not been sure if the boat was hostile, which was why he had been circling. He had just about decided that it was a boat-load of Allied prisoners, and was about to fly off when the Japanese gunner opened fire. Of course, he felt he had no option but to return the fire, with devastating results.'

Equally baffled is Mr. Harrison of Shorwell, Isle of Wight. 'This was a very strange experience of a coincidence which happened some years ago. It is not supernatural, but my wife and I thought it extraordinary.

'We had plans to move from Essex to the Isle of Wight, and because we would be moving to a larger house we needed extra furniture. We approached the firm of Redman & Hales of Hatfield Peverel, explained what we required, and they agreed to make the furniture for us.

'We decided to call to check the progress of the furniture making one day. Mr. Hales showed us an old watch upon which was engraved the words 'North Court, Isle of Wight'. Mr. Hales explained that he remembered me telling him that we were going to the Isle of Wight, and when he had picked the watch up in a sale a few days earlier, he recalled our conversation. That was what made him show me the watch, he just thought we might be interested.

'I replied, saying that I was not interested but amazed because North Court was the exact house which we had just bought. Mr. Hales told me that the watch was one of a verge movement, made by George Body in 1780 and was probably a gift to someone on the estate.'

chapter fourteen

FATE

The Tube

Deep in my eye I see a hole
I slowly change from man to mole
The more I do the more I find
Those buried questions in my mind.

As in a spiral tube it seems
With blowing wind and hazy beams
Like walking down a lamp lit street
No feelings come from hands or feet.

The tube seems large, it's huge to me
And still so dark, no floor to see
My body's gone – it's locked outside
Still in the tube, down I slide.

I journey on deep down I go
But just where to I still don't know
The whole new world is all around
And still no floor is to be found.

The sides grow wide like in a cave
My fear shows now I must be brave
I've come this far, I must go on
Through shadows, storms and raging sun.

Those sudden lights they hurt my eyes
Like comets lost deep in the skies
All around me doors appear
They look afar but feel so near.

And when I knock or open try
A sudden flash they're gone from eye
What's going on is this a game?
Open up – give me your name.

I move onto another door
Succeed with this I must for sure
Then as before it goes the same
Still no answer still no name.

I look around at every door
They're even on the roof and floor
And at the back I quickly see
There's one half open – swinging free.

I slowly creep up to this door
The buried secret's here for sure
But as I grab this open gate
I quickly feel I hold my fate.

Now what to do I must be sure
A sense of fear comes more and more
What happens if beyond I find
My fate and future in my mind.

Is it right to see this way
Or should it be from day to day
Dreams and hopes would be no more
Best I think is close the door.

And as I close the door up tight
All the others go from sight
I feel I've had a chance to see
What my future is to be.

And as I walk back through the street
All fields, so tidy, good, and sweet
From my visit to a world unknown
Fresh new thoughts and seeds I've sown.

I'm sure it's best never to find
Those hidden secrets in your mind
You never know I might just chance
To come again and take a glance.

Bob Anthony
Woodhall Spa
Lincolnshire

Bob Anthony was inspired to write 'The Tube' just a few hours after he suffered a heart attack. 'I lay there in bed and suddenly I saw what I could describe as a tube. I noticed that my feet were not on the floor any more and I was travelling or gliding down this tube. It was windy yet my hair stayed still. At the end of the tube there was a glow of silvery light. I carried on walking until all of a sudden the wall of the tube became covered with doors of all sizes.

'All of these doors kept opening and shutting apart from one. I reached this one door and I was just about to open it when a sudden fear came over me. I let go quickly and turned round. I honestly felt at that moment that if I had opened that door I would have seen my fate. I wasn't ready for it. I was too afraid. I know it sounds crazy, but I somehow knew it was my fate.

'I can remember how wonderful everything looked on my way back. Although I was still floating, there was now a visible pavement and there were trees, fields, and a fantastic bright blue sky. I observed my physical body as nothing more than an empty shell. In fact I still strongly feel that I exist in two parts, and that my material body is only here to keep the real part of me serviced and maintained.

'As I opened my eyes I saw a scrap of paper by my bed, and I instantly started to write the poem "The Tube". Now I have trouble trying to write a simple letter, let alone a poem. It took under fifteen minutes. I didn't plan it – it just seemed to flow out of the pen and on to the paper.'

Some things in life just seem to click into place without any effort whatsoever, yet when trying to instigate other events, no matter how much trouble we go to, the desired end result never happens. Could it be that some events are mapped out by fate and that certain people are fated to meet on this earth?

People might argue that if we have free will, how then can we believe in fate? Perhaps the answer lies in a mixture of the two. There are certain signposts marking our way along the pathway of life, in the form of events to be experienced, lessons to be learnt, tasks to be handled and people to be encountered, decisions to be made. Precisely how we deal with these signposts rests with us and our free will.

141

Nevertheless, some things just seem to happen out of the blue which change the natural course of events in a person's life in an inexplicable way. A gentleman of Letchworth, Hertfordshire, experienced something whilst serving in the Royal Auxilliary Air Force, Fighter Squadron.

'I was working as an aero-engine fitter at the time with my friend, who was an airframe rigger. We were feeling a bit low because we had recently lost our pilot, who had had a fatal crash in a Spitfire. Our new pilot was the best friend of the one who had been killed, and we were allocated to him as his ground crew. We had been re-equipped on the Squadron with new jet fighters, and one particular weekend the whole Squadron was on a big air defence exercise based away from our home airfield. However, my pal and myself were ordered to stay at base to re-fuel and service our new pilot's plane, while he was on a short leave as his wife had just had a baby. He had been permitted to fly back to see her and the baby briefly, then return, in a couple of hours, to the exercise area.

'Our pilot taxied in and stopped the engines. He got out and asked us to re-fuel with full tanks and check over the plane to have it ready to fly again in about an hour. He went off, telling us that the Form 700A was in the cockpit, under the parachute, in the seat. This was the special log book into which we had to enter all the servicing details and how much fuel we had put in.

'We carried out the re-fuelling and did the other between-flight checks as did the electricians, armourers and instrument mechanics, but when we came to sign up for all these little jobs, the log book was nowhere to be found. The Flight Sergeant was very angry about this, because to lose a log book in the Air Force was as bad as losing your birth certificate or passport.

'We searched every nook and cranny. We even took the parachute to pieces, then we took the complete seat out of the cockpit. As a last desperate resort, I felt that we should check the camera-gun bay which was over the nose-wheel. I took off the cowling panel and, to my surprise and great concern, there, wedged in the undercarriage retracting mechanism I found a one-pound hammer. The implication of this was that it would have been quite possible during the next flight, when some violent tactical manoeuvres were to be carried out, that the hammer would have jammed the nose-wheel in the up position – and on this type of aircraft it would have caused a particularly dangerous type of crash-landing for the pilot.

'I removed the hammer, put the front end together, and we put the seat and parachute back in the cockpit and resolved to tell the "Chiefy" that we had utterly failed to find the log book. At that moment the wireless mechanic came up to do his check. He leaned forward into the cockpit, picked up the missing log book, which was on the top of the seat which had just been refitted. "Is this what you chaps are looking for?"

'We were all stunned! The book just seemed to materialize out of thin air. Did our old first pilot have something to do with looking after his pal who was due to fly off in the plane? Had we spotted the book in the first place, I would never have found that hammer. I know what I think.'

During the Second World War, a young soldier from Newcastle was sent to Bournemouth on a mechanical course for three months.

'I had just been married for over a year and I remember I

143

distinctly had the feeling that all was not right at home, and that if I could only get up to Newcastle everything would be all right. I had the overpowering feeling to get back home as quickly as I could, but being in the forces it was absolutely out of the question.

'That night I went to sleep in my bunk as usual. I felt myself coming out of my body and rising up. I looked down and saw myself on the bed, and I realized that although my body was there, I was not part of it or, if you like, my spirit was not there.

'I remember the thought that came to me. It occurred to me that if I went to Newcastle, which I knew I could have done easily, would I be able to return to myself? The fear that I would not be able to get back to my physical body cancelled out the will to travel north, then I found that I was returning to my body. I was completely conscious of my re-entry. I just seemed to merge or blend into myself.

'Needless to say, I did not mention any of this the next day. Can you imagine the response I would have got from a barrack-room full of soldiers?

'When I returned to Newcastle, I learned the awful truth. My wife had, in fact, been having an affair with another man. Our marriage was dissolved, but I can't help wondering sometimes what would have happened had I had the courage to make that trip to Newcastle to check up on things. Perhaps we were fated to split up, who knows? All I remember is the intensity in my mind to get home to save the situation.

'It's funny when I look back on those days. I'm sure my life would have followed a totally different course. I have been happy in the way things turned out and I can't help feeling that it was meant to happen the way it did.'

A short example of fate can be illustrated by the story of a young girl, who for obvious reasons wishes to remain anonymous. She had just moved into a top-storey flat with her boyfriend of several months, much against the wishes of her parents. One morning, they had a blazing row, and the boy stormed out. She drank a full bottle of brandy and devoured a bottle of aspirins as well as some packets of flu-powder. The flat was three flights up, over a small parade of shops. The cocktail of brandy and aspirins acted on her system very quickly. All her thoughts blackened to despair. Her attention wandered to the window.

In a split second she ran to the window, pushed it up and took a nose dive straight out. As she fell head first, the heavy window clattered back down and pinned her by the ankles. She was held by her feet, and could not move up or down. She screamed and screamed and screamed. A passer-by rushed to the back of the building, broke into the flat and saved her life.

Had the window come back down a fraction later, or had she been a fraction quicker diving out, she probably would not have been alive today. Was this fate?

A young lady called Shirley from Dorset had just become engaged, and was sent on a training course to Birmingham by her company. She had only been in the city for a few days when she passed an old tramp in the street. She just glanced casually in his direction, while hurrying past him. Their eyes met.

'Something magical happened in that moment. As soon as our eyes met we both knew that we were in love. It's the craziest thing in the world, and if anyone else had told me that this had happened to them I'd think they were completely mad. There was an unbelievable fascination and attraction between us, yet were total strangers, apart from the fact that he was a filthy vagrant, the kind of person people cross the street to avoid.

'We kept staring into each other's eyes. I felt as if I was rooted to the spot. I couldn't move and I couldn't look away; nor did he. After what seemed like an eternity, he spoke to me. His voice was gentle. He smiled, and as he did I realized that he was not as old as he had first appeared to be. I think the wild beard and moustache, and his straggling hair, gave a false impression – but it was his eyes that held me spellbound.

'We fell head over heels in love, and had a sizzling affair. I was very apprehensive about my engagement, but every time I thought about my fiancé back in Dorset, I kept hearing a voice in my head telling me that everything would turn out all right. No matter how things looked at that moment, everything would work out and that I was not to worry.

'After two weeks, I received a message to go to the local hospital. When I got there I was told that the tramp had collapsed with a brain tumour, and he had died just before I arrived at the hospital. My phone number was in his pocket – I was the only contact he had in the world.'

Although she was devastated at the news, she knew in her heart that she had been fated to meet the tramp in the very short time he had left on this earth. She also had the overwhelming feeling that her relationship with him had been designed in order to help her overcome something – something which would affect her in her own future although, at the time, she had no idea of what that 'something' would be. She put her marriage off, although she remained good friends with her fiancé.

Four years after the death of the tramp, Shirley was given the news that she herself had a tumour and she was suffering from terminal cancer. Instead of the expected reaction of grief and despair, she found that she possessed an inner strength and determination to fight. She knew then deep within her soul, that her tramp was helping her through and her own illness was what she had been aware of four years beforehand.

She made a complete recovery, married her fiancé and has been happy with him, although she feels, beyond doubt that someday she will be re-united with her romantic tramp.

Many people claim that they fell in love at first sight, despite the levelling remarks of their friends who suggest that to talk about love at first sight is fanciful nonsense, and could not possibly happen. All kinds of explanations and theories are presented in an attempt to disprove the claim.

However, even the most cynical adversaries admit that there is such a thing as attraction at first sight, but love? Never! Others argue that it is all accountable in retrospect, and that because the couple eventually grew to love each other they became tricked into believing that their first feelings for each other were nothing less than true love.

There is evidence to show that claims of love at first sight may not necessarily be the idyllic ramblings of star-struck infatuated fools, but that this can, and does, happen. Sexual sensibility operates on energy at molecular level, which means that impulses are sent to the brain at very high speed – in fact, thousands of times faster than ordinary signals are transmitted by the mind. Therefore, people receive sexually-related messages in record speed because they by-pass the logical mind, which is far too slow to deal with such perceptions.

It is perfectly feasible that within a few moments of two people meeting for the first time, thousands upon thousands of messages are relayed between them at split-second speed, and experts say that the information relayed could be sufficient for the two people to weigh up everything there is to know about each other in a single instant.

The feeling of recognition when meeting certain people for the first time could be explained by the idea of collective consciousness, or group souls, whereby people tend to cling to their own kind.

A sympathetic bond connects the members of the group, and compels them to seek each other in whatever realm of existence they happen to find themselves.

Over two hundred years ago, a young girl called Jean Armour jilted her husband-to-be Robert Wilson, and wed another Robert – Robert Burns, a struggling tenant farmer, who was to become a household name throughout the world as Scotland's national bard. Now, another piece of history has been made – the Armours and the Wilsons have finally got together when their descendants, Karen Armour and John Wilson, recently married in the old town of Ayr. Karen is related to the bard's wife, Jean Armour, and John is a direct descendant of Robert Wilson, the 'Gallant Weaver', jilted by 'Bonnie Jean' and immortalized in song by Burns two centuries ago.

Karen admitted, 'John and I might never have got together if it hadn't been for our strange family histories. I have distant family connections with Jean Armour and John is the great, great, great, great grandson of Robert Wilson, the man Jean should have married if Burns hadn't "bowled her over".'

The couple met at a dance and John told Karen that he

was researching his family history, and was writing a book about the Wilson clan. He recalls, 'I knew quite a lot about the broken romance between Robert Wilson and Jean Armour, who had been his childhood sweetheart before the poet had come into her life. When Karen told me her surname, and that she was related to Jean Armour, you could have knocked me over with a feather.'

Karen added, 'I think Burns had a romantic soul. I believe he would approve thoroughly of two young people getting married and fulfilling the destiny that was planned for Jean and Robert Wilson so many years ago.'

There must have been a very special kind of love between Robert Burns and Jean Armour. That is the only explanation for her sticking by the side of her poet husband through thick, and mainly thin. She was the mainstay of his adult life and the woman he always returned to. In Edinburgh, his new-found glittering society told the poet that his Ayrshire roots were holding him back. They said he should abandon the Scots tongue and write in 'proper' English, but it was Jean who gave him the safe anchor, who bore his children and who nursed him devotedly through his last long illness, to the end.

John Wilson is doubtful if he will ever be able to express his love as beautifully as Burns did, but he proposes that a new line should be included in the wedding vow - 'And I will love thee still my dear, till a' the seas gang dry.'

One evening, Carol Reynolds walked into a smart hotel lounge bar with her boyfriend, and she immediately caught the eye of the young man who was tinkling away on a baby-grand piano. Her heart skipped a beat as she instantly recognized the handsome features but, try as she would, she could not place his name. The pianist smiled and waved across to her, then she instinctively walked over to him and told him how lovely it was to see him again. He replied unhesitatingly, 'Yes, it's been a long time, hasn't it?'

At this point, Carol's boyfriend interrupted the conversation by ushering her away from the pianist to a quiet corner of the bar. After a few moments Carol began to feel acutely embarrassed, saying to her boyfriend that she felt she had made a terrrible blunder, and that she must have mistaken the pianist for someone else. The feeling was so strong that she was compelled to approach the pianist and make her apologies to him. However, when she once found herself face to face with this stranger, she became even more convinced that she was not mistaken, and that deep down she knew him very well. Before she could utter a word to him, her breath was taken away by his remark, 'I suppose I should apologise for mistaking you, but I could have sworn that we knew each other.'

During the following months Carol and Tom, the pianist, became closer and closer, and when he asked her to marry him she accepted eagerly. They became engaged and a few weeks before the wedding she was invited to visit Tom's parents, who lived three hundred miles away, for the first time.

As they waited on the crowded platform for the train, Carol suddenly remembered that she had left her handbag in the Ladies' room. In a panic, she ran back to retrieve it, without taking time to explain to Tom what had happened. When she returned to the platform, she was just in time to see the train pulling out of the station, and to her horror, there was no sign of her fiancé anywhere. She stared in shock as the last carriage chugged further and further away from her, taking with it her whole world.

The painful days and months turned into years as Carol tried desperately to put Tom out of her mind. Eventually, she met a kindly, considerate man who proposed to her and she accepted, thinking that marriage would free her from the torture of her unrequited love. Although she was extremely fond of her husband, she learnt that the deep underlying pain was not erased as she had hoped, but it was becoming easier to live with. She had three children, and after a reasonably happy twenty-six years of marriage, her husband died. Four years later, encouraged by her family, Carol joined a pen-friend club.

One morning she was slightly bemused when she opened a letter from a new pen-friend, a widower with two sons, who signed himself Tom Patterson. She smiled sadly at the coincidence of receiving a letter from someone with the exact same name as her beloved pianist.

After a few more letters had been exchanged, the amazing truth dawned on Carol. Her new pen-friend was the same man who had broken her heart when he jilted her so many years previously, but because Carol had naturally been writing to him in her married name, he did not realize that she was the same person.

On answering a knock at her front door one day, Carol was surprised and shaken to find herself face-to-face with her ex-fiancé, who stood sheepishly holding a bunch of red roses. He had decided to introduce himself to his pen-friend. The astounded look on Tom's face told Carol that he instantly recognized her. His dark hair was greying at the temples, but apart from that he had changed little over the years. When his clear blue eyes gave her that old, familiar, special look, her heart melted.

They sat down to talk and Tom told Carol that he could

never understand how she had jilted him without warning, that day at the station.

'But you were the one who jilted me,' exclaimed Carol. They found themselves laughing at how silly they both had been, but then the laughter faded when they realized that their whole lives could have been so different, had it not been for that one misunderstanding. Each of them had been too hurt to contact the other to seek any explanation.

There is a happy ending to this story. Two months ago Carol and Tom became engaged to be married, and they are absolutely convinced that they were always meant to be together. 'It's as if we have always loved each other,' says Carol. 'Although we've both been married to other people, somehow we always knew that we were made for each other.'

Tom, a mature, practical man admits, 'I know it sounds ridiculous, but I feel I've known Carol since time began. It's the only way I can explain it.'

Bob of Oxford, a shy, rather awkward young man in his late teens, always found it very hard to attract girlfriends. 'I'm not much good at small talk,' he explains, 'And when it comes to chatting a girl up, I just get tongue-tied and embarrassed.' He worked as a junior accountant for a big company, and was dedicated to making a successful career, so after a few blind dates which had been arranged by his friend went disastrously wrong, he more or less resigned himself to the life of a bachelor.

One night, after he had been asleep for some time, something made him open his eyes. He became aware of a bright light in the corner of his bedroom. 'When I saw it first I was so puzzled I didn't know what to think. I wasn't afraid so much as bewildered. I could not take my eyes off this oblong-shaped, orange-coloured light which seemed to hover about a foot above the floor. As I gazed at it I began to realize that it was not just a light, but that I was looking at three forms. I suppose my eyes were gradually becoming adjusted to the terrific brightness, for at first I was just too dazzled to distinguish anything.'

The forms became more and more clear as Bob stared in disbelief. In the middle, there stood a woman in her late thirties with short, dark curly hair in a rather ordinary dress, wearing dark coloured spectacles. On her right side there stood a boy of about ten, and on her left a little girl of about seven or eight. All three of them were staring intently at Bob, who admits, 'I didn't recognize any of them, and I remember wondering why they were there and what they had to do with me. Funny though, when I think about it, there was no sense of fear. I didn't feel threatened in any way, just mystified, if that's the right word.'

All of a sudden, from out of the silence, Bob heard a strange voice announce to him, 'These are your wife and children.'

'I felt thunderstruck,' recalls Bob. 'I remember thinking to myself that it must be some kind of weird joke. The woman was years and years older than me, and she appeared more like a mother than a wife. The next second everything vanished and I was left staring at the bedroom wall. I remember looking at the clock, and it was past three in the morning. It certainly wasn't a dream as I was wide awake. I even got out of bed and went downstairs to the kitchen to make myself a cup of tea.'

Bob's life continued as usual and nothing remarkable happened, until one day over two years later when he literally bumped into a girl on the stairs at work. She was a new secretary who had just started the previous day. Bob turned to apologise to the girl, and the moment his eyes met hers, he heard a voice repeating in his head 'This is the girl – this is the girl.' He was totally confused by this voice because the young girl called Susan was a glamorous blonde and looked nothing like the woman who had been shown to him – no spectacles, much younger, even different coloured hair.

Within the next few weeks, Bob found that he was able to talk to Susan very naturally without the usual self-conscious feeling which he normally got with girls. She was vivacious, pretty, good fun to be with and, most of all, she made him feel at ease. They started dating and, after a short courtship, they agreed to get married.

All of this happened over twenty years ago, but the incredible thing is that today Susan looks exactly like the woman in Bob's vision. She now wears glasses – with thick dark rims, she has allowed her hair to go back to its natural colour – dark brown, and she has put on some weight since her children have been born – yes! – two children, ten year old Michael and little Julie who is nearly eight.

'It is so unbelievable when I look at Sue and the kids,' says Bob. 'Their faces are exactly the same as I was shown them all those years ago. I could understand it if I had known someone who looked like the woman in the apparition but, at that time, I knew nobody like her at all. It really is uncanny how things work out.'

chapter fifteen

ESCAPE

The release of the spirit from the physical body frees the wandering soul from the natural limitations and restrictions of being trapped in the body. People have likened it to a prisoner being set free from solitary confinement. All the hampering conditions of flesh, blood and bone have no longer any effect on the spirit. One of the main differences which people constantly remark upon is that when they are out of their material bodies they feel no pain whatsoever, yet that is not because 'feeling' is not experienced. On the contrary, they report that they felt 'wonderful', 'happy', 'exuberant' and a string of positive conditions.

It is interesting to note that, apart from fear as a result of the initial shock of finding themselves out of their bodies, very few people have reported anything other than a feeling of extreme well-being.

Because human beings feel pain as a direct result of messages relayed to the brain, due to a change in our physical tissue, then it follows that when we are not clothed in our material bodies we cannot be subject to these conditions which brought about the change. It also follows, therefore, that it is impossible to feel pain once the spirit has separated from the body.

Some human beings seem to have a built-in safety mechanism whereby, under certain conditions when they are in severe pain, an escape is engineered by the spirit slipping out of the body. Many women have reported that this happened to them during childbirth. It is documented that some prisoners-of-war had the same release when life became unbearable in the cells.

A woman from Tamworth in Staffordshire was informed by her doctor that she had a cancerous tumour. 'The pain was getting more and more intense, and I was really struggling to get on top of it. Last year things became unbearable, the pain was absolutely unbelievable. On many occasions I used to drift out of my body when I just couldn't stand it any more. I would sit on the other side of me, and I was able to see how ill I looked. To be quite honest, I sort of knew I was facing death. It was as if I could no longer stand the pain in my body, and during those moments I had taken a little time out of it.

'I didn't dare tell anyone about this, as I am certain I would have been sent to the madhouse. All I'm saying is that I knew that I was able to escape from the brunt of that pain when it all got too much for me. It is now a year after my chemotherapy, and I am doing quite well.'

Angus Dudley of Bedfordshire remembers how he had a narrow escape when, as a boy, he had been out playing with his friends. 'It was one moonlit night, shortly after Christmas when the ice on the village pond was two feet thick. It had snowed on top of our slides, so we chopped a hole in the ice and spread water over the snow, so that it would freeze over and give us a smooth surface.

'Later around 9.00 p.m., I went back to the pond with my friend, John, and as the water had not yet restored the surface sufficiently to make a reasonable slide, we thought up a new game. We took a stick each and started to play putting, by using a piece of ice instead of a ball. We took turns in getting the piece of ice into the hole which we had dug previously.

'When we ran out of pieces of ice, I squatted at the side of the hole to pick some out and I fell headlong into the hole. I remember sinking into the icy pond, slipping down and down, with columns of green water rushing past my eyes. Then I started to float back up to the surface, but instead of remaining there, to my surprise, I kept floating right up out of the pond and into the air, lying face down on nothing. When I was about ten feet up I watched my friend put his arm into the hole in an attempt to find me. He was peering down into the dark water, fishing around with his hand and, at the same time, trying to prevent himself from toppling into the water. I could see him struggling, then he put his other arm into the water. I saw that he had got hold of something which, I then realized, was my hair. He pulled frantically at the hair until he managed to drag my head above the surface of the water.

'I drifted down to give him a hand, yelling for him to try to get a hold of my shoulders, but he took no notice of me. I shouted louder and tried to grasp at my sodden clothing, but I found that my hands could not form a proper grip on my jacket. The next thing I could feel the freezing water all around me. I opened my eyes and found that only my head was above the water, and I could see the dark elm trees on the bank of the pond, silhouetted against the sky. The cold was excruciating, so I started screaming loudly then, with John holding my collar, I managed to climb out of the hole. I ran home and dried off, and I did not even catch a cold.'

When Mr. Paul Bright of Warley in the West Midlands was a small boy, living with his parents, he was constantly the victim of bully tactics by a boy called Stan, who was three years older, a bit taller and heavier.

'One day Stan had been playing at my house and, as

usual, he started to bully me. He had pinned me to the floor and was literally strangling me. I was terrified because his grip was so strong on my throat that I could not even shout for help. The next thing I knew I was floating near the ceiling.

'I remember looking out of the window as I was bemused at being able to see out from so high up in the air. However, instead of the normal sights which I should have been able to see outside the window, I could only see a cloud like a fog and there were no sounds whatsoever. At this time I did not realize that I had left my body. It was only when I turned and looked down that I guessed that something odd was happening, because I could clearly see Stan, with his hands still pressing on my neck. He and my own body seemed to be in the distance, although we were all in the same room.

'I felt as if I were extremely small, although I was quite happy with the situation and was not in the least afraid. I turned my attention back to the window, then I thought that I'd better investigate this cloud of fog, so I tried to move closer to the window to have a better look. I was stopped from moving to the window by what felt like heavy hands on my shoulders, preventing me from moving. No matter how hard I tried to wriggle free from this grip, I could not shake myself away from it. It was as if the hands were turning me round to make me look at how Stan was strangling me. I did not want to watch, but the hands kept turning me, so that I was forced to look down instead of going towards the window, which I still wanted to do. I was completely indifferent to what was happening to my physical body.

'I then realized that the hands which I could feel pressing on my shoulders were trying to push me back down into my body. I struggled even more to get away, and towards the window. I could now see Stan slapping my face, I had passed out on the floor, and I think he had started to panic. At that moment I felt the mysterious hands give me an almighty push, which sent me rushing towards the floor and into my own body.

'A draining sensation swept over me, which started at the top of my head and crept all over my body. I could hear Stan asking me if I was all right. I told him what had happened but he just laughed at me and left. I told my two cousins about it and they also laughed at me, so I did not mention it again.

'When I was in my twenties I read an article in the paper about people having OOBEs, and it was only then that I recognized the similarities, and realized that that was what I'd had all those years ago, When I think of it, I find myself shaking slightly, or shivering as if I were cold. It all seems so vivid, unlike other ordinary memories which tend to become a bit hazy.'

A distraught battered wife found escape from the clutches of her irate husband's hands by slipping out of her body. 'My husband regarded me as a chattel to vent his frustrations on. One day, when the children were toddlers, they had been playing with his tube of toothpaste. This infuriated him so much that he came storming into the kitchen, roaring at the top of his voice. He had a dreadful expression on his face and I honestly thought he was going to kill me.

'He rushed straight up to me and put his hands around my throat. I was absolutely terrified, but then fear was my main emotion at that time in my life. I said, "Lord, help me," then immediately I was up on the ceiling looking

159

down. I was at perfect peace and could see both of us standing by the stove, his hands still round my neck. The feeling of freedom from fear was such a relief that I truly did not mind whether I went back or not.

'I watched from above as my husband relaxed his grip on me, then I felt myself floating back down into my body. I was never afraid of him again, as I was not now afraid of dying and to kill me would be the worst thing he could do to me.

'I was a battered wife for ten years. I put up with it purely so as not to disrupt the children's lives when they were so young. After we divorced he married someone else in the village, but by all acounts he is not too happy with his lot (as ye sow, so shall ye reap). He wanted to come back to me shortly after he left, but he would not undertake not to hit us all, so I couldn't have him back.

'I wonder if other people who have left their bodies feel, as I do, that death is nothing to fear.'

chapter sixteen

CHILDREN

It is accepted that some young children are acutely perceptive, particularly before school age. Perhaps this is because their minds are not overbusy with the demands of organized learning, therefore they are more receptive to incoming influences, the lines of communication being comparatively clear.

Many children can give elaborate details of memories of what seem to be previous lives, in places totally unknown to them, and in words beyond their normal limits of vocabulary. In our book entitled *The Children That Time Forgot* (Sinclair) we document cases of this phenomenon.

One little girl remembers her previous existence as a boy who lived in a remote Yorkshire village over one hundred years ago; another child remembers stark details of her funeral when she had previously died as a child of only five months old; yet another child recalls what happened when he drowned after falling over the side of a sailing boat; a girl remembers being one of the child victims in the Tay Bridge Disaster, when a Pullman train plunged into the black, icy waters of the River Tay in Scotland.

There are countless reports of children having seen ghosts, very often the ghosts in question being other children. There is a distinct lack of fear on the part of most of these children, and they accept what they see as being perfectly natural. We have all heard of some child who has an invisible 'friend'. This friend is normally referred to in affectionate terms. No doubt, some children are living in a world of make-believe in which the invisible friend fits perfectly. However, there are often cases not as easily explained, whereby there really does seem to be more in it than meets the eye.

A lady from Oxford moved into an old house with her husband and little boy of three years of age. 'The house was always cold. At first we thought that there must be something wrong with the central heating system. We had that checked and we were assured that there was no problem with it. However, even when the radiators were hot, the rooms for some unaccountable reason remained cold. I just couldn't understand it, so I just put it down to the fact that because the house was old, perhaps there was damp in the walls, which our surveyor must have missed or overlooked.

'Then the noises started, all kinds of thuds and thumps, but we could never find any reason for these. I used to watch my little boy like a hawk, wondering if he was getting up to mischief but several times I heard the noises upstairs while my little boy was downstairs with me, my husband was out at work and I was certain that there was no-one else in the house. I noticed that the noises, sometimes like footsteps or running feet, seemed to be restricted to certain areas – the stairway, landing and my child's bedroom. Sometimes I would hear a dragging sound as if something was being pulled across the floor of my little David's bedroom.

'It got so bad that I could hardly stand it. My imagination ran riot and I became convinced that we had either rats or bats in the rafters. We got in a specialist company to go over the entire house. We even had the floorboards removed in all rooms, including David's room, but there was nothing to be found.

'Still the noises continued. They began to sound like

162

footsteps on the bare floorboards. This just didn't make any sense at all because the entire house was carpeted wall-to-wall, including the stairs. One day, from upstairs, I distinctly heard a child calling out "Mummy". I, of course, assumed that it was David calling me, but I knew that he was out playing in the back garden. I could see him from where I was standing. He was playing up and down the garden path with a little red truck, which had a rope attached to it. As I watched him, again I heard the word "Mummy", and it definitely came from upstairs.

'I rushed up as fast as I could, thinking that some neighbouring child must have somehow wandered into the house. I passed no-one on the stairs, and when I got to the top there was absolutely no-one there. I searched every single bedroom, the bathroom, and I even looked in the linen cupboard on the landing, I was so certain that there was a child in the house.

'I began to wonder if my nerves were playing me up. After all the strange noises, perhaps I was beginning to imagine things.

'Several nights later, in fact at precisely 2.30 in the morning, I was awakend by a voice calling "Mummy". I naturally got out of bed to go and check on David. To my surprise I found him sitting up in bed, wide awake with all his toys around him. I remember saying to him, "What are you doing with your toys at this hour?" He beamed up at me. "I've been playing with John." I tucked him in and didn't think too much more about it until a few days later when I went to my next door neighbour's house.

'I didn't know her very well because we had only recently moved to that area. There happend to be a photograph album on the neighbour's table. She saw me glancing down

163

at the album and she invited me to have a look through it. Now, if there is something I hate doing, that is looking at other people's photographs, especially those of strangers. However, just to make conversation, I turned over a few pages of the album while my neighbour put the kettle on to make us some coffee.

'One photograph struck me as rather odd. It was of a child in a pram, but what drew my attention to it was that the child looked far too big to be in a pram. He was a boy of about five years of age and would have been on the large side, even for a push chair, let along a proper pram built for small babies.

'As I was looking at this photograph, my neighbour came over to me. I didn't like to say anything, but took it for granted that the child must be a relative of the woman. She smiled and said, "I suppose you know about him." I shook my head, then she went on to say, "They used to put him in that pram because he would get so tired. You see, he had cancer." Still assuming that she was speaking of her own relative I asked who the child was. She answered, "Oh, it's little John who used to live in your house. He died in there when he was only five." A cold chill went through me at her words, and everything started to make sense.'

Stephen Worthington remembers an experience he had when he was only five years old. 'Sudden and unexpected though it was I will never ever forget it. It happened late one winter's night on my fifth birthday. I had been playing with my toys on the upstairs landing, when a model car slipped out of my grasp, tumbling down the stairs. I leaned over the top of the stairs, watching in horror as my favourite car lay smashed to bits at the bottom of the staircase. I leaned over a bit further to get a better view and I slipped. I realized my mistake but it was too late. I fell over and bounced down every one of those steps.

'I reached the bottom, badly shaken, but not hurt and felt myself drift off into a deep sleep. After what seemed like a few passing moments I felt myself out of my physical body, hovering at a distance of about two feet, then floating back up the stairs until I reached the landing at the top. By some strange force I was gently placed down onto the landing with the delicacy of a feather floating down onto a velvet cushion.

'I felt completely weightless and as I looked down the stairs at my own corpse I noticed that I was wearing a little white jacket, trousers, tie, shirt, socks and shoes. I just stared at myself at the bottom of the stairs for a few moments, trying to comprehend what had happened.

'Then I jumped in the air and found myself floating towards the attic. I kept moving in that direction until I willed myself down again.

'Soon afterwards I saw my mother and my aunt enter the downstairs hallway from the living room. They saw me lying unconscious, and rushed towards my body to pick me up. The next thing to happen made my heart freeze; my aunt sighed, brushed away a tear and said, "Oh my God, he's dead!" At this my mother started crying uncontrollably, both of them weeping over my lifeless body.

'At this point, my father and uncle rushed into the hallway to see what was going on. They found the two women crying over my body. My uncle consoled my mother and my aunt, while my father examined my body to see what had happened. I then watched him carry me into the living room.

'I got a bit fed up watching them, so I wandered along the upstairs landing into my grandparents' bedroom and passed a tall, floor-mounted mirror. I thought I'd better check my appearance in the mirror to see if the fall had made any cuts or bruises on my face. To my confusion, the mirror reflected back absolutely nothing, even though I was standing right in front of it. I blinked, pinched myself, stared and even made silly faces to see what would happen, but still there was no reflection.

'I moved back out onto the landing and looked down the long forbidding staircase, and in a burst of enthusiasm I jumped from the very top of the stairs and arched myself into a diving position, then proceeded to fly down the stairs. I was just like Superman!

'For the next few moments, I can only say that the feeling I experienced was extremely beautiful and memorable. After flying at an even, gentle speed, I finally reached the bottom, then I felt myself re-enter my own body. The next thing I knew I was wide awake, sitting on the sofa in the living room, surrounded by the grown-ups.

'They asked me how I managed to fall down the stairs. I was too confused to answer, because I wasn't sure if they meant: how did I fall down the stairs or how did I fly down the stairs? Everyone around me was in a most joyful frame of mind due to my sudden recovery. Today, eighteen years after the event, my parents still remember it and are still baffled at how I made such a rapid recovery. As far as they were concerned I was dead and my father found when he had checked my body there was no trace of heart-beat or pulse.

'I know it was real and not a dream, and it is an experience I shall never forget, nor, I think, will my parents.'

Mrs. Rosina Drury of Dunstable told us her moving story of the child she lost. 'Shortly after our little son was born we were given the terrible news that he had cancer in his eyes and that he was almost blind. It was a dreadful shock to my husband and me. The little boy, whom we had named Paul, was admitted to hospital and went through the gruelling ordeal of having one of his eyes removed in a desperate attempt to save his life. Sadly, my little boy did not make it through the operation and died in the hospital.

'Our other child was only two-and-a-half years old, and she could not understand where he had gone. She kept running to fetch his nappy and powder, saying that she wanted to help me change him as she had always done. She kept asking me to let her cuddle him.

'I could not bring myself to tell her that Paul had died. One day I got her ready to take her out. At that time we lived in a ground floor flat in Leinster Gardens, Bays-water, in London. The sun was shining in through the kitchen window. Suddenly, she pulled at my skirt saying, "Mummy, Mummy look." I did not take a lot of notice as I was cleaning round the sink. Again she pulled at my skirt and said, "Mummy, look, there's Pauly!" I couldn't believe what I was hearing, so I looked down at her instantly and there she was, looking and pointing to the sky.

'I looked up, but could not see anything. I put my arms around her and said, "Where is Pauly?" She was adamant that she could see her little brother. She kept pointing to the sky. I asked her what he was like and she said, "He's not as big as me. He is standing by a big goldy gate. It is all shining and he had got all golden curls just like me. Look,

167

there he is." For the life of me I couldn't see him, but I am convinced that she must have seen something. The thing was we had hardly spoken about him, it was too painful.'

When Mr. James Harbottle of Wallsend, Tyne-and-Wear, was only four years old he was rushed to the Fever Hospital on the Burnfield. He was placed in a bed near the window in a serious condition, suffering from the multiple effects of diphtheria and scarlet fever, further complicated by bronchitis. Both of his parents kept a bedside vigil, and it was feared that the end was near.

'I remember lying quite peacefully. I must have been oblivious to everyone in the room as it seemed silent and empty to me. I was occasionally aware of seeing a nurse hovering around the bed. I remember clearly, however, when I started to drift out of my body. I just drifted in the air around the room, then I went towards the window. At first I thought that I'd better be careful not to crash into the window, which I could see was closed. To my amazement, I found myself floating right through the panes of glass and out into the garden.

'There was a pathway and as I moved along I saw a tall man with a long beard. He held out his hand to me and although I did not know him, I moved towards him. I was not afraid, nor was I particularly curious, I suppose I just went because he beckoned to me. He then lifted me up in his arms. When I looked back through the window into the hospital room I saw that both my mother and father were crying. This upset me very much, and I just wanted to rush back to them to comfort them.

'The man did not say a word, but I could see him watching my parents. He seemed to understand so he opened his arms and let me drift back through the window towards them. When I was back inside the room I looked out and saw that he was still standing there. He raised his arm and waved to me. I remember waving back at him, then the next sensation was of waking up in my physical body, gazing up at my parents. They seemed pleased to see me, and kept hugging me.

'I seemed to get better quite quickly after that and soon my parents were wheeling me home in a borrowed push-chair. It was the first time I had ever been in a push-chair, so I was quite pleased with myself. I was taken to visit my granny who welcomed me with more hugs.

'Whether it was the spirit of a man or God who held me, I cannot judge. I've since heard it said that when young children die, the spirits of their dead ancestors look after them. Certainly after my own experience I know that children need have no fears.'

chapter seventeen

FEAR OF DEATH CONQUERED

Eternal Life

There was no secret key, we scarcely felt
Our final passage through the closing door;
Our only pain was knowing people knelt
Wishing their world of doubt on us once more;
They loved our shadows, and the sun was gone,
They have no eyes to see how we remain.
Nor can we point them to a peaceful dawn
Where blindness sees, and sorrow smiles again.
We have discarded names, waves in a sea
We move to other shores, being as one,
Beyond our fear we find a unity:
As one life ends, another has begun.
We are no longer casualties of clocks,
Death gave us life: we know no paradox.

Frank McDonald

On sifting through the thousands of out-of-body cases, one overpowering conclusion keeps coming to light again and again. It does not explain what causes astral projection but it does point to the effect such experiences have on almost every person on their return to their physical bodies, they no longer fear death.

Mrs. Dorothy Bush of Abington, Pennsylvania, USA, feels that she has completely got over the fear of the unknown, from which almost all of us suffer, since she had an unforgettable experience just before her second child was born.

'I had a fainting spell in the examination room of the hospital, and the doctor felt that it would be best to perform a Caesarian section. While lying on the operating table and having a conversation with the anaesthetist, I felt as though I was going to faint again. I told her this and she gave me some oxygen, which did not help. The last thing I remember was her yelling to the doctor to hurry, that my blood pressure was falling.

'I then found myself in this beautiful place. I knew it was Heaven: so peace-filled, so beautiful, and such beautiful music and beautiful flowers. Although I could see no-one, someone started to talk to me, saying, "Dottie, I am leaving you on Earth for a purpose; no-one will know what you are going through". He proceeded to make known to me *all things*.

'I felt, as he talked to me, "Why did he choose me to reveal all things to?" And then I thought that since he did, now that I have had this convincing experience, I can be of help to others by helping them to understand. Then I thought about his words, "No-one will know what you are going through." I wondered then if this meant that upon returning to Earth I would not remember what was revealed to me. I was most conscious of this fact and I remember going over, in my mind, what I had just been shown, so that I would remember it all.

'When he finished talking to me I felt myself floating away from that beautiful place to a dirty, ugly one, so great was the contrast between Heaven and Earth. I did not want to return, although he said that I must. I then felt myself back in my body on the operating table.

'My doctor told me that resuscitation measures had been required because of apnoea and hypoxia, which translates, I understand, as cessation of breathing and lack of oxygen in the brain. I then felt the doctor putting tape across the bandage on my stomach but I could not open my eyes. Someone was saying The Lord's Prayer, and when they said "Amen" I opened my eyes as though I had just had a nap.

'I was taken back to my room, and told my husband and Mom that no-one would know what I had just gone through. I said I would not complain again about anything. Although my resolve faded with time, I did eventually become more patient with everyone and everything. I always had believed that there was life after death, but having been there and returned, I certainly found out for sure.

'That night, as I lay on my bed, I tried to remember what had been revealed to me, but I was unable to. I knew deep in my heart that I had been shown wonderful things. I have never been able to remember the revelation, but the experience remains vivid and convincing as when it occurred.

'I have gone through some testing and trials in recent years, but I know that they are lessons which must be learned here on Earth. I find myself led to certain places, or drawn to certain experiences at times, and I look upon life in a completely different way since I had my experience. The helping of others and the love that we should have at all times for others, this is what we are here for. It is a great frustration to see others running about with self-centred attitudes and activities that are such a waste of their lives. What I am trying to say is that seeing so much unthinking selfishness in the world just makes my heart ache.

'I have met others who have had the benefit of the near-death experience and they too long to share with everyone the lesson of this higher consciousness and love. I have no fear of death. I actually look forward to going home when God calls, for I know "the best is yet to come".'

Another lady who, like Dottie, was giving birth when she slipped out of her body, Mrs. Jean Norman from Aberdeen in Scotland, says, 'The baby was very overdue, and the doctor was worried about the birth. He gave strict instructions that he was to be called in immediately after I went into labour, since I was having the baby at home. However, my labour was such that the nurse did not dare leave me, even to telephone the doctor, so my husband had to help her.

'After a very difficult time, my baby boy arrived almost dead because the umbilical cord was wrapped so tightly round his little neck. At the moment of birth I found myself floating up to the ceiling. I looked down at my body on the bed, and I could see the nurse shaking me and slapping my face. My husband just stood silently staring at me and the baby who was lying on the bed with me.

'I felt as light as a feather, with no pain whatsoever, such a contrast to the terrible agony I had suffered while I was in my body. I had a wonderful feeling of happiness, and I knew that I needn't ever go back, it was as if I had a choice. I thought to myself that it was so peaceful where I was that it was much nicer to stay there. Then I looked down at the three figures below, and I felt such pity for them. In an instant I was back in my body.

'When the doctor arrived, the nurse told him that she thought she had lost me as I had died just as the baby was being born. I felt no fear of death as I am quite sure we only pass through a door. Previous to that experience I was as scared of death and dying as most people are.'

A date in the beyond was what brought Mrs. Phyllis Wilkinson of Bolton, Lancashire, the conviction that death is nothing to fear.

'I had not been widowed very long when one night I thought I had woken up. It was in my mind that I had made an arrangement to see my husband, although I was fully aware of the fact that he was dead. I felt my spirit (or whatever it was) rise up and leave my body, feeling sure I was on my way to see him. I might add at this point that I am not religious.

'I hovered for a while close to the ceiling, and looked down at my physical body in the bed. I noticed the exact position I (or should I say "it") was lying in. I then remembered that I had to meet my husband outside my old school, so I just floated through the closed window without even hurting myself. It was as if I was flying over the rooftops until I arrived at the outside of the school. Seconds later I saw my husband coming towards me. My mind was clear and I was able to think in perfectly logical terms. As soon as I saw him, I thought that I would have to treat this situation with great care because although I knew he was dead, the exuberant way in which he came rushing towards me told me that he must not realize that he has died, so I would have to choose my words carefully so as not to alarm him.

'We started to walk along, chatting happily, but after a short time, he kept saying that he was cold, so I knew it was time for him to go. I then found myself back in my bedroom, to see my physical body still in the exact position

174

it had been in before I'd left. I just slid into it. It was like sliding into a glove. I then said to myself, "I'm going to wake up now" and did just that.

'I have not told many people about what happened because I think that they would scoff and say it had just been a dream. If it was, it was the most vivid dream I have ever had. In fact, it was a shattering experience which I will never forget. The one sure thing is that I know I will see my husband again, and I have no fear whatsoever of what lies ahead as I am convinced that we all meet up with our departed loved ones.'

For a family man in Belfast, the horror of horrors happened one day when he was shot in an assassination attempt. When his unconscious bleeding body was found he was rushed to hospital and straight into the operating theatre. He regained consciousness and screamed out in pain. He asked to be given something to ease the pain, but was told that he could not have anything until it was decided what was to be done. 'They were worried because I had just had lunch and they had to be careful about what they gave me, so at that point I had been given no drugs whatsoever.

'Suddenly I became aware of someone standing by the side of my bed. I turned my head but could see no-one, but I still had the overpowering feeling that someone was there beside me, a male supreme being. I heard the words, "I'm in charge, everything's O.K. There is nothing to worry about." The moment I heard those words I felt all the fear just leave my body. I could distinctly feel as if a wet blanket was slowly being drawn off my body, I could actually sense the drawing out of the fear from me. I never would have believed it could happen like that. I felt the close proximity of this being and felt engulfed with peace beyond belief. I knew that I would recover and that everything would be fine.

'My attitude to death has changed greatly since then, because I now know that we are never left on our own at any time. There are beautiful good people there who help us through and who are filled with love.'

A lady from Belfast, Trudie Watson, returned home after an enjoyable holiday in the Isle of Man. She felt a bit off colour and did not take too much notice of this. But things deteriorated fast and Trudie found herself in the Fever Hospital, completely paralysed with polio. Being a brave young lady of 25, she asked the doctor to level with her, and asked him what were the chances of her recovery. The doctor could see that she really wanted the truth, so he informed her that she had 24 hours to live!

That night she woke up in the hospital. Being completely paralysed she had been placed in a cot on her back, and the nurses had firmly tucked the bed-clothes in all round. She could only move her eyes, but her brain was completely alert and active as normal.

Suddenly she found that she could sit up in the cot. She thought that this was strange, and then she wondered if perhaps the medical staff had got her records mixed up with someone else's. Then she remembered the dreadful pain in which she had been, and the fact that she had only been able to move her eyes. She became confused because there she was, sitting up in the cot, with every trace of pain gone, and yet she was supposed to be paralysed. She then felt herself move up and away from the cot.

'I just kept floating lightly, like a feather, up and up, until I was about nine feet off the ground. I found myself lying on a black wooden plinth, just like a door without a handle on it. I remember observing that because the wood was so black it must be ebony. I looked down and startled myself when I saw my still body lying in the cot, still all tucked in the way the nurses had left me.

'The plinth, with me lying on it, started to move towards the door. I was not in the least bit afraid. As I got to the door, I heard the cry of a young child. I knew this was not my child's cry, but it immediately reminded me of my own little boy who was only two. The second I thought of my small son I was right back in that useless body again, tucked up tightly in the cot.

'I recovered fairly quickly after that because I had the intense will to survive to look after my child. The doctor told me that I had been drifting in and out of heart failure while I was in the cot. Even though it was a dreadful illness I would not have missed it for the world because I now have not the slightest fear of dying when my time actually comes. So much for the 24 hours to live! I feel as fit as a fiddle and am still going strong.'

A Birmingham gentleman, relates how he was going through an unpleasant emotional period with his lady-friend. 'As I sat in my chair, trying to sort out in my mind the reasons for her unreasonable and unpredictable behaviour (which was the cause of my anxiety), I was unknowingly staring at the wall (fixated). There were long gaps in between my thoughts (one might say daydreaming, where the mind wanders off doing its own thing) and it was during one of these blank spaces that I could actually feel the life force flowing into my body, and as my body filled with this spirit, I became consciously aware of a feeling of peace (well being). I was completely alone, yet something hit me very hard on the back of the neck; I believe it was then that my eyes closed and I experienced a pleasant sensation of "sinking down". A voice occasionally called my name (Derek) and whenever I repeated my name silently to myself, I enjoyed further pleasant sensations of "sinking down". Another two strong hits on the back of my neck each sent me deeper and deeper within myself. I think the sensation of being hit was probably the procedure for releasing my inner body because I found myself floating just below the ceiling and looking down at my physical body sitting in the chair. I could actually move around to different parts of the room and look at myself from different angles. I could move in or out of my body at will, I had no fear, because it was a natural feeling. I felt perfectly free and happy with not a care.

'I instinctively knew that my inner self (or spirit) was indestructible, so when I heard a bus in the street below, I flew through the closed window and, knowing that nothing could harm me, lay in its path; the bus passed over me easily and I quickly returned to my body. The speed with which I could move was fantastic; I remember being quite pre-occupied with speed at the time and the next thing I knew, I was shooting from my body through the top of my head, and powering my way through the ceiling and the flat above. I did not think about my body sitting in the chair and felt rather sorry at leaving it, but this was only momentary. I went through the roof and continued at terrific speed in an upward direction.

'There was a mist which suddenly parted to reveal a place

where colours were transformed by an unusual quality of light, where the sun, stars and planets appeared bold, stark and real, but for me the feeling was of peace, light and love.

'I remained there with my arms outstretched, looking towards the sun, and noticed that my whole body was shimmering in the light. I had no hands, face or feet, and with my arms outstretched, I appeared to be like the "Cross of Peace".

'This place has many names, but none of them quite apt: Christians call it Heaven, Buddhists call it Nirvana and Red Indians call it the Happy Hunting Ground, but whatever it's called cannot reveal its subtle nature. Mystics say it is pure bliss, infinite love and all-embracing unity.

'My out-of-the body experience changed my life considerably, and I am now no longer afraid to die.'

A shorter account of how she overcame her fear of death comes from Mrs. Hall, again of Birmingham. 'It happened shortly after my father died. I was very upset because I had always felt that he had not received attention early enough.

'Anyway, I saw myself lying in bed. I had somehow or other released my true self from my physical body. I started to float down a long dark tunnel which was growing brighter and brighter. I stopped about half way along and, in a brilliant light, I saw my father, sitting in his wheelchair. He smiled broadly, waved to me and put his thumb up as if to say that he was O.K. I turned and started to travel back down the tunnel.

'I know this sounds ridiculous, but I will always believe it. My father convinced me that death is nothing to worry about.'

A sad story comes from Carl, a blind man of 23 years of age, who rang in response to one of our radio phone-in programmes to tell of his experience. It convinced him that death is nothing to worry about.

'I am blind and gay, and had been living with another young man who was also blind. My friend was dying. He had brittle bones. We both knew the score and we tried to be philosophical about it. One day I had the sensation that I was flying, and for some reason I got the impression that he was in New York. I was still blind and could see nothing, but because I could "feel" the high buildings I came to the conclusion that I must be in New York. I'd never been to New York before, in fact I'd never been out of England. I had the distinct impression that my friend was with me.

'I don't pretend to know how this happened, and I would not know where to begin to explain it. I only know it happened. I have often thought about it, and ever since it happened the panic everyone feels about dying just left me. Sometimes I even wish that I could be taken away to be with my friend again, because I depended on him so much in every way. I suppose we depended upon each other. I am certain that we will be together again in the afterworld.

In the *New York Times* of Tuesday, 28 October 1986, the following article was published, entitled 'Near-Death Experiences Illuminate Dying Itself'.

The mystery of death haunts the living, but real understanding of it has always proved elusive. But researchers say new studies of people who have come close to death and show it may be less painful, less frightening and more peaceful than it is generally conceived to be.

These conjectures are derived from near-death experiences of people who came close to death or were revived from a state of clinical death, usually after a painful accident or illness.

According to Kenneth Ring, a professor of psychology at the University of Connecticut, people undergo a 'brief but powerful thrust into a higher state of consciousness' when they are near death. Many people who reach this state describe their experiences in vivid detail. Many report the feeling of travelling through dark tunnels towards a bright light; a few report floating above fields of yellow flowers.

'One definite finding of the research is the diminishing fear of death from those who have had these experiences,' said Karl Osis, former executive director of research in Manhattan and an author of a book on near-death experiences.

Dr. Osis and other researchers say people who have had such experiences may help relatives or friends to face death.

Near-death experiences vary in length and intensity, but follow roughly the same pattern. People who undergo them report feeling abrupt separation from their bodies and looking down upon themselves. Their pain dissolves, they say, and they are overwhelmed by an inexpressible peace and contentedness.

Many say they enter a tunnel of darkness and move towards a brilliant white light that emits warmth and love, and they are flooded with knowledge beyond their ordinary capabilities, so that they discern the pattern or meaning of life.

A Gallup poll reported that 8 million people have had near-death experiences and found that no relationship existed between the experiences and a person's religious or cultural background. Studies have shown that children have these experiences.

John Migliaccio, a New York business executive for a publishing and consulting firm, had a near-death experience in 1968 when he almost drowned off New Jersey. While swimming towards the shore, he became over-tired and said he felt himself leave his body and hang 500 feet in the air, 'like being in two places at one time'. He kept on swimming as he felt he was actually watching himself in the struggle to survive.

After reaching the shore and blacking out, 'I just let go', Mr. Migliacci said. 'I went straight into this blackness, travelling what seemed like a million miles a second. I went up into this great void. The only way I can describe it is that I was part of everything in the universe. Everything fit together and made sense to me.'

The experience changed his attitude towards death, he said. 'A year before, my grandmother died and I went hysterical.' But when his grandfather died a year later, 'I felt inappropriate, everyone was upset but me.'

According to Bruce Greyson, an associate professor of psychiatry at the University of Connecticut, and editor of the *Journal of Near-Death Studies*, no physiological or psychological theory explains near-death experiences.

Some scientists have suggested that the dying secrete endorphins, hormones that act on the central nervous system to reduce pain and which are otherwise associated with 'runner's high'. Endorphins cause effects comparable to those of morphine and may cause hallucinatory experiences.

But people who have these experiences deny that they were simply hallucinations. 'It was a real experience,' Mr Migliaccio said.

While experts say near-death experiences have been recorded for centuries, only in the past decade have they begun to gain credibility in scientific circles.

Leading the research is the International Association of Near-Death Studies, which Dr. Ring and several other researchers founded five years ago, and which is based at the University of Connecticut.

According to Dr. Ring, near-death experiences are a catalyst for spiritual development, the individuals seem to become more self-confident, less materialistic and more giving of themselves. People who have these experiences often believe they have escaped death to fulfil a special mission in this life.

Such was the case of Virgina Sendor of Hempstead. Mrs. Sendor had a near-death experience in 1960 when suffering from uremia. 'I knew I came back for a reason,' she said, 'but I had no idea what the reason was.'

But in the late 1970s she began working with terminally-ill patients and their families. By 1983 she realized it was her mission to open a hospice on Long Island. So Mrs. Sendor founded Long Island Foundation for Hospice Care and Research Inc., which provides a range of counselling and support services to patients and their families.

'I know now this is what I'm supposed to be doing,' said Mrs. Sendor.

Researchers say those who have near-death experiences can share their views of death to comfort others.

Geraldine Divito of Mt. Laurel, N.J., had a near-death experience in 1978 when she had an allergic reaction to medication. Two years later, her husband was diagnosed as having pancreatic cancer. He died three years later. Mrs. Divito believes that she helped ease the pain that her husband would otherwise have suffered.

'I know there was nothing to fear,' she said. 'I had that little glimpse into the life-after death.'

chapter eighteen

PREMONITIONS

We received many reports from people who have had flashes of events which, by our reckoning of time, were scheduled to take place in the future. Some of these events were quite trivial but some have come in the form of definite advance warning of catastrophe. The people who experience such premonitions feel most frustrated because even if they could pin-point the origin of the catastrophe they feel they would not be believed.

A Coventry man, Mr. Pemberton, had a lucky streak one day. 'It started with a stretching feeling, being drawn out of myself, so to speak. I found myself arriving in a hall and hovering above some people who were about to draw some tote numbers. I watched from above as they turned the barrel and drew out the winning numbers, number six followed by number nine. The numbers were written on ping pong balls. I felt like an all-seeing eye and was surprised they could not see me. I was drawn back into my body, woke up and promptly made a note of the numbers six and nine. For some reason the number forty-two kept ringing in my head. This confused me as I had not seen that number during my escapade in the hall.

'Anyway, later that week when it came to selecting numbers for our tote I played my hunch and told the collector that I would bet on those numbers. I had never been lucky in the tote before so I did not give the matter any further thought.

'A few days later my friend Arty Harper, my confidant at the time and the only person on this earth that I had told about my strange experience, came rushing up to me, eyes all alight, saying, "You'll never guess, the numbers nine and six have won, and there were forty-two winners." It was a very small pay-out that week, but to me the money came second as something more valuable came out of it. By the way, I checked with the collector to ask exactly how our work tote was drawn as I'd never really been that interested in it before. I was told that the numbers were all on ping pong balls and they were picked out of a barrel.

'I think I have been very lucky to have experienced this insight or whatever it was. I know that I am not unique as I have heard of many people who have had similar experiences. I never got any more 'tips' after that, anyway I'm not really a gambling man.'

Mrs. Thelma Trenchard of Falmouth in Cornwall had a premonition when she was staying at her mother's home 'Ivy Cliff' near Falmouth, although her own home, at that time, was in Oxford. 'It was just a quick flash in a dream in which I saw our two youngest children, Colin and Nesta, out on the river in our small boat. I saw Colin bump his head on something.

'That was all there was to it, but when I woke up in the morning, just as my mother's housekeeper was coming into the room with a cup of early morning tea, my hand was shaking so much that I could hardly hold the cup. Although the rest of the dream had been vague, my sense of danger was alerted and I was overcome with a feeling of fear for the children.

'I suppose it felt worse because I was so far away from my husband and children, who were all at home in Oxford. I had been called down to 'Ivy Cliff' to attend to some of my mother's business. I telephoned my husband straightaway, but he put my mind at rest saying that the children were fine and that there was nothing to worry about.

'The following day I received an urgent telephone call from my husband, who was very upset. He explained that there had been an accident, but the children were safe. It had happened after my husband had set off for work that morning. Nesta, Colin and their friend had decided to take our boat out on a backwater of the Thames. Colin had bumped his head on a low bridge. They lost an oar overboard and broke the outboard motor. They had been in grave danger of being swept down a weir which was in full spate below them. Luckily there were other boats on the river and several people came to their rescue, and they were pulled to the safety of the bank.'

Scores and scores of people have reported the Lockerbie plane disaster days before it happened. Some of them felt so strongly about it that they tried to contact the officials of various airlines, but of course without more concrete evidence they were not taken seriously.

Deep in the Welsh vallies there lies the little village of Aberfan, which will forever be remembered because of the terrible tragedy which wiped out almost all of the tight-knit community's children. A landslide caused the local school to be buried under tons of earth and slag from the nearby mines.

Mrs. Williams, a young mother from the North of England, was most disturbed when she had a vivid dream of a landslide in a village area. In the dream she saw a gravestone, on which was marked the name 'Anne Williams'. She was most distressed as this was her daughter's name. She was filled with a terrible sense of foreboding, and was sure that something was going to happen to her little girl.

186

A few days later, she was sitting at home watching television, when the News was broadcast of the disaster. It was reported that the schoolteacher was also killed. Her name was Anne Williams.

chapter nineteen

DANGERS OF THE OCCULT

All of the experiences described in this book are of a spontaneous nature. At no time did any of the people mentioned take part in any form of psychic formula or ritual in order to release themselves from their physical bodies; nor did they consume any drugs, apart from the cases under medical supervision in hospital.

The dangers of involving yourself in the occult cannot be overestimated. To experience true spiritual perception is one thing, but to purposely set out indiscriminately to seek involvement in the paranormal, by whatever means happen to be at your disposal, is asking for trouble.

Let there be no doubt about the point we are making here. Avoid all involvement in *ouija boards, fortune telling, tarot cards,* and especially any form of magic whether black or white. Although these things may have a degree of novel fun about them, they are extremely damaging to the spirit, because their origins spring from Satanic influences.

Some people might argue that these practices must be all right because they work. How many times have we heard people swear by this or that clairvoyant, often to the degree that no important decisions are made without first consulting the clairvoyant.

From our research, we can state that for the most part it does not work. Most of the so-called clairvoyants utter inconsequential drivel, made up as they go along, mostly based on their acute observations of the unsuspecting person who has parted with his or her money. The clairvoyant is often little more than a pseudo-psychologist, playing with people's emotions and abusing their vulnerability. Within seconds of meeting your run-of-the-mill fortune teller, she will have weighed you up, taking into account your appearance, your accent, your stance and deportment, the texture of your hands and the rings on your fingers, if any, the expression on your face, your general attitude. After a few key questions, which most people react to even if they don't realize it, she has her clues to progress further down the road of deceit. Even if you purposely do not react to her initial questions, this, in itself, tells her a lot about you.

We unearthed a training school for clairvoyants on the south coast, and they unwittingly admitted to us that the entire reading is done by nothing less than trickery, in as much as the questions are framed in such a way as to guarantee feedback (however subtle) from the subject.

After one or two visits to such people, or after one or two sessions with the ouija board, it takes only the minutest degree of success to warrant more and more involvement. This does not even sound logical, and in fact it isn't. Logic has nothing whatsoever to do with it, such is the charismatic effect that sudden power has on most innocent individuals. Every tiny succcess is magnified in the mind beyond all recognition.

Just think of this. How many people have told you that they have dabbled in the occult in some way or another, either by visiting a clairvoyant or by taking part in a seance? They probably told you excitedly about the one main factor which 'came true'. Did they ever mention all the other hundreds of factors which did not come true? Most probably not! That is because the negative factors die a natural death in the mind, whereas the one thing that 'came true' dominates the mind in a totally exaggerated manner, thus giving a distorted sense of importance to that one success, blotting out the hard fact of all the other failures.

This strange deviation from the normal workings of the mind is caused by our inner need to believe in something more than that which we can see with our physical eyes. The problem is that in dabbling with the occult, we are tapping into the wrong source – the negative source – rather than the positive source from which true enlightenment flows.

Everything can be reduced to simplicity. Things are either good or bad; positive or negative; for or against; beneficial or detrimental. Even the grey areas which would initially seem to fall between these firm borderlines can be analysed down to fit into one category or the other. There is really no need to complicate things by assumptions which cloud any particular issue. Therefore, it follows that the occult must also fall into place like everything else in creation – it is either good or bad, positive or negative.

The questions then arise, how can we tell for sure? How do we know whether the occult is good or bad? The answer to these questions can be found by examining the evidence. Without exception, people who embrace the occult (usually either for fun, to start with, or as a last desperate resort to find peace and happiness and reassurance in their lives) do not truly find what they are looking for. They still have to face the same old problems, but added to this is the burden of fresh worries, which often lead to a general sense of hopelessness and disappointment with life in general. In extreme cases people become suicidal.

If you have been dabbling in the occult, ask yourself honestly, have you recognized any of the following tell-tale signs creeping into your life: excess anxiety and fear;

emotional instability; severe depression; an overpowering feeling that life has become almost too difficult to cope with; overindulgence in food and drink; profound feelings of inadequacy and failure; inability to get on with other people. Are you consumed with feelings of self-pity? Is there discord within your own family? Is there the threat of a break-down in your marriage, or symptoms of nervous disorder? Do you feel utter frustration in everything you attempt, leading to neurotic tendencies?

If you are affected by any of the above conditions it could well be that you are suffering from some form of Satanic oppression, either physically, mentally, spiritually or on a psychic level. Because of your wilful involvement in the occult, you have exposed your soul to demonic power and invited evil and negative influences to enter, causing total havoc in your life.

Remember, Satan exists. He is real. He can, and does, influence unsuspecting souls, very often by the most subtle, undetectable means. He is the essence of deceit, and only after you have been well and truly conned will you waken up to the fact that nothing beneficial has come your way since your involvement in the occult.

However, there is hope! Even if you feel you are suffering from any of the aforementioned afflictions, all is not lost. In the time it takes to blink your eye, you can transform your whole life. It only takes a fraction of a second for a thought to enter your conscious mind and relay its message to your brain. The thought which you must introduce to your brain is this: 'I totally and wholeheartedly renounce all evil and negative influences and forbid them to affect me in any way whatsoever.' There! The deed is done! You have freed yourself from Satanic influences.

The overpowering point to grasp is this: by the laws of creation, it is a fundamental fact that evil is secondary to good. Therefore, an evil thought or influence can never, under any circumstances, dominate a pure positive thought or a good influence. Negative thoughts and influences can only have an effect when they meet up with their own kind. Remember, like attracts like!

From this, it is easy to see how a snowball effect occurs by one negative influence feeding upon another, and growing in intensity until the force of negativity attacks the negatively-inclined person with soul destroying vengeance. This can be illustrated by mob violence at football matches. The forces which originate in evil are allowed to run riot, inciting violent feelings to manifest themselves. The excuse is a game of football. How pathetic!

Evil is often cloaked in the most clever disguises, such as in organized cult groups and, in some cases, even orthodox religion. How many misguided souls have set out to fight wars, deluding themselves that they were fighting for their religion? Surely this is a contradiction in terms. Any religion worth its salt should surely preach love. If it does not, something, somewhere is amiss!

Once you have made the conscious decision to reject all evil influences from your life, you have overcome the first, and most difficult hurdle. You have recognized the problem. The next step is to take the necessary action to prevent any further Satanic evil forces from affecting you. This, you may find, will take courage, but remember that good thoughts *always* win over evil, therefore do not lose heart. The reason for needing extra courage at this stage is that Satan and his followers do not give up easily. As soon as they feel they are being opposed you will become aware of the following sensations: you will begin to have second thoughts about your recent decision to exclude all negative influences from your life. This is the typical procedure for undermining your own confidence in your ability to shake off the negative forces. Deal with this as follows: repeat your resolution to forbid all evil and negative influences to enter your life. Even if you are faint-hearted at the prospect of repeating this, do it anyway.

For once in your life be firm with yourself. You will be hesitant because you will start to feel silly about the whole thing. You will have to deal with thoughts giving you the false impression that you are running away with your own imagination. One way or another the doubts will surely creep in. Please recognize these doubts for what they really are. It is a sure fire sign that you have started to upset the Satanic applecart. You are on a winning streak, so stick with it. Show Satan who's boss. Defy him and repeat again that you totally denounce him and all he stands for. As long as you adhere to your good, positive thoughts, he can't touch you.

By now, you will feel a lot lighter in spirit. Positive influences are starting to break though. You can test whether you are on the right track by observing the following: you will now be smiling and even laughing, something you have not done for years. You will really score in the spiritual stakes if you laugh at him and his devious little tricks. You are now mightier than him by far. You can look down on him. He loathes to be ridiculed so why don't you treat him with the contempt the creep deserves?

At this stage, something wonderful will happen to you – something that no amount of money can ever buy: the fear will leave you and it will be replaced by true peace of mind. You will start to feel happier, you will be contented within. You know you are on top of things. The problems that of late have worn you down will gradually disappear. This will come about because your own attitude will have changed. You will be able to see things clearly, as they really are, instead of living in a dazed world of wishful thinking. You will become less self-centred. You will start to make correct decisions. Your judgement will no longer be impaired by negative influences. You will have courage. Your health will improve. You will look radiant and your eyes will shine from the light within your soul. Your relationships with other people will bring you joy. All doubts and feelings of inadequacy will vanish. Life will be beautiful and worth living. You will feel your spirit soar within you and praise God to be alive.

By now you will have created a protective shield of goodness around you that it will be impossible for any evil influences to penetrate through this to your spirit. You have won!

A fascinating development will be apparent at this point. You will now be able to look back on the times when you had dabbled in the occult, and you will see it for what it really was – a complete and utter waste of time and energy. You will see clearly the connection between your past problems and your involvement in the occult.

The next step to take is to ensure that you do not relax your defences and slip back to your old ways. Destroy all occult literature (if you have not already done this), including all occult tools, charms, medallions, instruction manuals, and all associated objects: everything, plus all the contact phone numbers, names and addresses, should be burned. This act, in itself, will further strengthen your protective shield.

All forms of witchcraft, in particular, must not only be avoided but positively rejected, be it presented to you as white, black or anything else. Make no mistake here – it is all Satanic, it is all of evil origin and can only lead you to unimaginable pain and suffering.

The hoard of so-called white witches will be up in arms upon reading this. Their argument will be that they do not practise all the dreadful things black witches involve themselves in. The white witches, in some ways, are more dangerous than their black counterparts, because they have developed deceit to a fine art. They will lure unsuspecting people into their midst by raving on about how they are only interested in nature, herbs, flowers, how they want to save the trees, etc. Don't we all love the flowers. The trouble is that they will not give you the complete picture. They use an incredible soft sell approach, but once they have you under the influence of evil, the rest of the sordid story emerges.

Up and down the country, in the suburbs and back alleys of quiet little England, the most grotesque, repulsive practices are going on. In the book *Witchcraft Conspiracy*, (Sinclair) the extent of this horrific situation is clearly shown. The problem cannot be underestimated. The evil must be stopped! We must unite in positive prayer to God, the only source of good, to bring about an overpowering force into the hearts and souls of each and every person who is, has been, or is contemplating involvement in witchcraft of any description. Evil will only prevail as long as good decent people do nothing.

If you have never before in your life stood up to be

counted, now is your time. There is something positive which can be done to eliminate such Satanic horror from our earth, and every thinking responsible person must do it.

We do not ask for money. We do not ask for anything. We beg you simply to consciously state the following: 'I wholeheartedly reject all Satanic influences from my own life and from the lives of all people living on the earth.'

With such a defence mechanism the witches, in their egotistical craving for power over others, will be wiped out. It truly is as simple and as instantly effective as that. Can you afford not to try it?

For any unfortunate readers who find themselves trapped because they have become involved in witchcraft and are too afraid to try to break free, there is also hope for you. Please have the courage to call a halt to your involvement. Chances are, if you face up to things and explain to your spouse, your parents, or whoever, they may well be sympathetic to your cause. Most decent people will see your need for help. You may well be in for a pleasant surprise. After all, what could be worse than your present Satanic imprisonment?

To employers, spouses, parents, teachers, social workers, medical staff and, indeed, to all people in whatever walk of life, please recognize this appalling problem and if you know of, or are faced with, anyone who is trying to escape from the clutches of witchcraft, for God's sake be sympathetic.

chapter twenty

PSYCHIC AROMAS

It often happens that people become aware of a presence in a room, not by seeing any person or entity, but by recognizing a scent which reminds them unmistakably of one particular person.

One man from Lincolnshire can always tell when a family crisis is about to occur as he always gets a strong smell of tobacco, the blend which his beloved late uncle always smoked.

"It never fails, every single time I get the tobacco scent something traumatic happens. It is always something highly personal and closely related to the immediate family. It is as if he is trying to warn me. He always succeeds in alerting my attention, but the only trouble is I can never quite work out exactly what is going to happen. The tobacco aroma has come five times already. The first two or three times I did not pay much heed to it, although I was acutely aware that it was the exact same smell as old Uncle Bert's pipe. Then, when events started to follow the scent, usually within two or three days, I started to wonder about it. When it happened the fourth time I remember thinking, "Here we go again, I wonder what it will be this time." I got myself into quite a state because there was no way that I dare tell any of my family, for fear of frightening them. Each time the youngsters went out on their bikes I found myself growing anxious about them, and when my wife was shopping with the car I was like a nervous wreck. That particular time, in fact, my wife did have a spot of trouble with the car, but thankfully it was nothing too serious –

someone knocked the bumper. I had mentioned to her before she'd left to take special care and not to take any chances. I suppose if I had not been aware of Uncle Bert's warning I might not have cautioned her in the way that I did, and who knows?

"It's a blessing in disguise, I suppose, but I can't help feeling that old Bert is trying to take care of us in the same way as he did when he lived with us."

Pipe tobacco lingered in a London flat even though Mrs. Watton, who had just taken up residence there, did not smoke. She scrubbed and cleaned, disinfected, polished and scoured but the pipe tobacco persisted.

"It was as if it kept coming in intermittent waves. I used to open all the windows but no matter what I did the tobacco smell was always there.

"I found out that the former tenant was an elderly man who had died in the flat, but at that time I knew nothing about him. One night I woke up suddenly and I distinctly noticed the room was very cold and, as usual, there was the strong smell of pipe tobacco. I then heard the front door bang, so I got up and went to look out of the window but I could not see anyone outside or on the pavement. The same thing happened again on two other nights at 1.00 am. The upstairs tenant was a retired nurse and when I told her about the tobacco smell and the front door banging, she told me that she had helped to look after the old man, and she said that he always smoked a pipe. She advised me to contact a priest, which I did. He came to the flat. I did not see exactly what he did, but from that moment the tobacco smell vanished and I have had no problems since."

Yet another story of tobacco aroma comes from a lady in Hyde in Cheshire. "Way back in 1957 my father died suddenly from a heart condition. He lived with us and I worked at the same firm along with him. When we had office picnics, about three times a year, he always came along with us. He was always last out and he would stand in the hallway, light up a cigar and then, when everyone was out, he would lock the door.

"A few weeks after he died, we were going to the Lake District on one of our office picnics. I was standing in the hallway with some of my colleagues. Suddenly I got a whiff of cigar smoke. I looked around quickly to see who had just lit up but, to my surprise, no-one was smoking anything. One of my friends was staring at me intensely, but said nothing. Later on I questioned the friend, asking why he had given me such a peculiar look while we had been standing in the hallway. He replied, "To be perfectly honest, I could swear that I could smell cigar smoke." I smiled, partly with relief and admitted, "So could I."

The same thing happened on three other picnic days, all in the hallway, just before we were about to lock up the offices. It was just as if my father was somehow reminding us to be sure to lock up before we left for our outing."

A bereaved husband was given consolation by the sweet smell of perfume. He was living in a state of numbness just a few days after his wife's death. "She was lying in a Chapel of Rest in Sevenoaks. I had arranged to visit my brother some miles from my home. I duly drove from my home to his, and as I passed through Sevenoaks the air was filled with the scent of perfume. I used no scented preparations myself. I do not use any scented materials in my car, my wife hardly ever used perfume, and certainly not recently, and I had not given anyone a lift around that time. The aroma only lasted for seconds, and it was not until I was passing out of

199

Sevenoaks that I realised that the scent arose at almost the exact time I had passed the Chapel of Rest where my wife was lying. I have a very keen sense of smell, but retracing my journey I cannot think of where the smell came from.

"My wife and I were very close. In addition to the normal man and wife relationship we were great friends, and I can't help wondering whether that once, because of our closeness, there was a brief attempt at contact."

A Lancashire lady believes that her dead husband has attempted to communicate with her and prove himself as a mystic medic.

"After my dear husband died quite suddenly, I felt him so near to me at times. Once when I was ill with Asian flu I suddenly became aware that my pre-fab was smelling of Friars Balsam. Now, Harry, my husband, had been a firm believer that this cured all colds and flu. I did not have any of it at home at all since I'd never bothered to buy any since his death, but nevertheless the whole place reeked of it.

"My son came home and remarked that I had been very heavy-handed with the old "FB", but I protested, telling him that I did not have a drop of it in the house. "But Mum," he persisted, "The whole place stinks of it." I found myself smiling sadly at my son and reminding him, "You know, Roger, your Dad was such a believer in old "FB". The smell lingered for three days and nights and then went as suddenly as it came. I do think maybe Harry was trying to let me know that he was still caring for me, even though he had passed over."

Great Yarmouth is a thriving, happy seaside resort, with all the fun and amusement one associates with a holiday town. The last thing we would expect to encounter in such a place would be a ghost. A woman from Norwich had a strange experience when she went there.

"I had just moved to Great Yarmouth after my marriage breakdown, and after several weeks I was allocated a council maisonette on Ordnance Road. As I was moving in, a young man who lived a few doors down said, "Hello, are you moving in? I hope you know that place is haunted." Taking this as a childish prank I ignored it. I installed my son's bed in a small room at the top of the stairs.

"At about 11.00 pm I went to bed. About 11.30 pm the bathroom door began to open and close, slowly at first but then faster and faster, and louder and louder. Thinking that I must have left a window open and a draught was causing the disturbance, I got up to investigate. There were no windows open and try as I might, I could not make the door creak as it had been doing. I went back to bed and I started to nod off to sleep.

"Again I heard the sound of the bathroom door opening and closing furiously. Again I got up, but as soon as I approached the bathroom, the noise stopped and the door was still. I went back to bed and just as I was almost asleep, the same thing happened again. By this time I was so exhausted after having just moved in that I just hadn't the energy to get up again, so I fell asleep.

"A few days later, my son and I went to stay with a friend for a week. When I came back I was greeted by a very unhappy neighbour who had two small children. She complained strongly to me about all the noise we had been making in the flat, banging and moving furniture about all the time. I explained to her that we had been away for the entire week, so it could not possibly have been us.

"The next day the flat was full of the smell of roast beef

emanating from the kitchen. That night, about 11.30 pm, I was reading in bed and I heard shuffling at the bottom of the stairs. To my horror, someone appeared to be walking, almost dragging themselves, slowly up the stairs. I leapt out of bed and ran to the landing, expecting to find a burglar or a drunk. The stairs were empty, but the laboured breathing continued as did the sound of the stairs creaking as someone invisible walked up them. When the noise reached the top of the stairs it stopped.

"This performance was repeated about three times a week for about a month. One night my son, who was 8 years old at the time, came screaming into my room and told me, "Someone's just kissed me and tried to pull the bedcovers over my face." I went into his little room and there was a loud buzzing noise (like a bee), not coming from any place in particular. Needless to say, I moved his bed into my room and we lay awake, listening to breathing, shuffling and buzzing the whole night.

"About a month or so later, I was talking to an elderly gentleman, and in conversation he happened to ask me where I lived. When I told him, he looked amazed and said, "I know it well. I used to court a lady who lived there, but she's dead now." The lady in question had been called Jane Cowper, and had suffered from a very bad heart. She had been taken to hospital to have a heart valve replacement.

"The small room which was my son's bedroom had often been occupied by her two nieces, whom she invariably put to bed and kissed goodnight. Now apparently her operation had not been successful and, one day, while she was cooking Sunday dinner (roast beef) she mentioned to one of the neighbours that she felt ill. The neighbour sent for the doctor and Jane went back home, and managed to pull herself slowly up the stairs. She reached the small bedroom and died there before the doctor arrived. The date of her death was 29th July. The haunting started about 20th June and reached a climax on the date of her death, then slowly faded away at the end of August.

"Every year after that, on the anniversary of her death, I used to move my son out of his small bedroom and into mine. I used to lie awake listening to repeats of Jane Cowper's last journey up the stairs and into the small bedroom.

"I did a little research into the previous tenants (none of whom stayed too long) and I discovered that many of them had heard Jane. One of them had requested a transfer because Jane had materialised in front of her little girl who had occupied the small bedroom."

chapter twenty-one

ANGELS

When we think of Angels we visualise perfect beings with beautiful faces and butterfly wings, and we usually associate them with sweet heavenly music.

This visualisation of angels may not be far from truth as many people have reported seeing creatures which fit our pre-conceived notion of how angels look, as Mrs. Fawcett of Yorkshire will confirm, although the angel she feels she saw had no wings.

She woke up one morning as usual, put on her dressing gown and hair net. "I felt as though I were walking round in slow motion. I felt awake but everything seemed hazy. I could see people but they couldn't seem to see me. I kept thinking I must go back to bed and wake up, but I couldn't. I could see my daughter asleep in bed but I couldn't get back in, so I walked round again. Then I was in this strange house, there was a pile of records and a man was looking through them. There was a book mixed in with them, the man pulled it out and asked who had put it there. It was a thin book, blue or grey in colour, with the word "Who" written on the cover.

"There was a table in the middle of the room, with a tablecloth on it. In the centre of the table was a jug which seemed to be full of cider. I couldn't understand what was going on. I went back upstairs but, no matter how hard I tried, I just couldn't get back into bed. Then I was walking in a white mist. The building I saw was also a brilliant white. I saw two long white steps on which sat a young girl, who had long fair hair with a parting in the middle. I walked up to her and asked her if I was dead. She smiled and shook her head. I was crying and she put her arms around me. I felt very cold when she did this and started shivering. I'm sure she said something about "Rusty" and that two came over but one didn't make it. Then I woke up feeling cold, although I was still covered up in bed with my daughter asleep at the side of me. It took me ages to get warm again."

Looking back on her experience, Mrs. Fawcett remembers, "When I was crying it was not because I was frightened, it was because I thought I was dead and I didn't want to be – not just yet, anyhow. All I can say about the girl is that she looked serene, very pale complexion, long straight fair hair with a parting down the middle, no fringe. She wore a white dress, no sleeves, and it had a low round neckline. I couldn't see the bottom part of her because of the mist rising from the ground, what with the steps being white plus the building behind her, which I could just make out – being white also everything seemed to mingle with each other. She just looked at me and smiled as if to say "Don't be afraid". I've never seen the girl since, to my knowledge. I don't know who or what "Rusty" is. When she said something about two coming over but only one made it, perhaps I was one of the two, I just don't know. Having said that, she gave me this message, although she didn't speak the words like we do. She just sat smiling, but I got the message just the same and she seemed to know what I was feeling. The worst thing was the terrible cold I felt when she put her arms around me. I'll never forget that. I liked the girl – she must have been in her early twenties, and she looked as though she hadn't a care in the world, serene is the only word for her."

When Mrs. Green of Derbyshire was about to give birth

to her son she had the most wonderful encounter with – not just one – but six angels.

"I had an extremely long and painful labour. However two hours before he was born I suddenly felt as though I were leaving my body and floating up the the ceiling, where I turned and looked down on my body. I could see everything going on – a tortured body and the staff all helping – one particular sister bent over me to sponge me down and the back of her hair parted to show a tiny curl.

"The next thing that happened was my body turned upwards and what was the ceiling parted and became the most beautiful blue sky with floating white clouds. My body started to rise and either side of me were three angels – the music and atmosphere were so beautiful and peaceful and I wanted to go. Somewhere in the background a voice said, "We're not going to get this baby in time". This must have made some impact on me as the voice got louder and louder – the angels and the blue sky floated away and I was back on the labour table. Somehow I got the strength to carry on and my son was born.

"The following day the sister who had sponged me down came to see me. My experience came back to me so I dropped something on the floor and she picked it up – yes, her hair parted and there was the little curl. I was very frightened and thought I was losing my mind, so I said nothing, not even to my husband.

"A few months went by and this experience was constantly in my mind, so I told my husband who reassured me I wasn't losing my mind. I also spoke to a friend about it. She seemed to have heard about this sort of thing and said when you're close to death you sometimes get experiences like this. I have had operations since and been very poorly but have never experienced this again. It still stands out very vividly in my mind and every time I hear anything about this sort of thing both my husband and I think back to that time."

On recapping upon her meeting with the angels, Mrs. Green recalls that they were positioned three on either side of her, one above the other with herself in the middle. "They were dressed in long white Grecian style gowns, their hair a golden colour. Everything seemed to be gold and white apart from the blue sky. As I floated upwards towards the sky I was being drawn slowly upward by a golden rope. There was sweet gentle music in the background – no talking – just an aura of peace and gentleness. When the sister's voice penetrated my brain that the baby might be born dead her voice got louder and louder until I screamed "NO". At that moment the angels started to float away from me higher and higher until everything faded away and I found myself back on the labour table – the ceiling was intact just as though nothing had happened.

"I feel the experience made me strong enough to carry on through the excruciatingly painful birth. It was as if I was given a rest from the pain, as if to catch my breath, but the impression left on me after my flight with the angels was so strong that it completely changed my whole life. I seemed to be filled with the joy of life and when, shortly after my return to the labour table, my baby son was born well and healthy my feeling of joy surpassed everything.

"The only sad thing about the whole episode was that the sister with the kiss curl on the nape of her neck died shortly afterwards while still only a very young woman."

There is a recognized hierarchy of angels which range from the mighty archangels, the chief one being Michael down through the seraphim; cherubim; principalities; authorities; powers; thrones; might and dominion (Colossians 1:16; Romans 8:37). There is some confusion amongst theologians as to the thrones, might and dominions, principalities (sometimes referred to as princes) and authorities. There are some who say that these are really all belonging to the same group and vary only according to the amount of power delegated to each of the types within the same group.

There is agreement, however, regarding the upper realms of angelic identification. The Archangel Michael is looked upon as being the highest of all angels. The name "Michael" means "Like Unto God". The feast of Michael is celebrated on 29th September as Michaelmas Day, and in 1950 Pope Pius XII declared St. Michael the Archangel to be the patron of policemen. Going back to the Old Testament, it was Michael whom God sent to protect Moses in his task of leading the children of Israel out of Egypt and into the Promised Land.

It is believed that in the last mighty battle between the forces of good and evil, Michael with his legions of angels will clash head-on with Lucifer (the fallen archangel) and his satanic followers. According to the scriptures, Michael will be victorious over Lucifer, hell will tremble and Heaven will rejoice and celebrate. It is Michael who will accompany Jesus at his second Coming and with a mighty booming voice he will awaken the dead – "For the Lord Himself shall descend from Heaven with a shout, with the voice of the archangel . . . and the dead in Christ shall rise first." (Thessalonians 4:16).

Gabriel is sometimes referred to as an archangel, but some say he is a unique personage of angelic substance who acts as the messenger of God. The name "Gabriel" in Hebrew means "The Mighty Hero".

It was the angel Gabriel who appeared to the Virgin Mary and announced to her that she was to become the mother of Jesus. It is not hard to imagine how a young girl would be most startled when suddenly being confronted by the awesome sight of Gabriel in all his splendour as he declared to her, "Do not be afraid Mary; for thou has found favour with God. And, behold, thou shalt conceive in thy womb, and bring forth a Son, and shalt call His name Jesus . . . And He shall reign over the house of Jacob for ever; and of His Kingdom there shall be no end". (Luke 1:30-33). Mary's answer was simple and to the point, "Behold the handmaid of the Lord, be it done unto me according to thy word." (Luke 1:38).

When Zacharias was in the temple the angel Gabriel appeared to him to tell him that his wife Elizabeth was to give birth to a son who was to act as a forerunner of the Messiah, preparing the way of the Lord. Zacharias questioned this for the fact that Elizabeth was advanced in years and well past child-bearing age. "And Zacharias said to the angel, "How shall I know this for certain? For I am an old man, and my wife is advanced in years." And the angel answered and said to him, "I am Gabriel, who stands in the presence of God: and I have been sent to speak to you, and to bring you this good news. And behold, you shall be silent and unable to speak until the day when these things take place, because you did not believe my words, which shall be fulfilled in their proper time." (Luke 1:18,19,20). Because of his doubt, Zacharias was struck dumb. It came to pass that Elizabeth did indeed give birth to a baby boy (John the Baptist) and it was only after the birth of the baby that

Zacharias' speech was returned to him. The first appearance by Gabriel took place when Daniel was in prayer, "And behold, standing before me was one who looked like a man. And I heard the voice of a man between the banks of the Ulai, and he called out and said, "Gabriel, give this man an understanding of the vision." (Daniel 8: 15,16). Gabriel went on to explain to Daniel the events which would take place at the end of time.

The seraphim are primarily concerned with love and are constantly glorifying God, being situated above the divine throne. In Chapter 6 of the Book of Isaiah we are given a description of the seraphim . . . "Each having six wings; with two he covered his face, and with two he covered his feet, and with two he flew. And one called out to another and said, "Holy, Holy, Holy, is the Lord of Hosts, the whole earth is full of his glory."

Next in importance come the cherubim. In the book of Ezekiel, Chapter 10 it states, "Then I looked, and behold, in the expanse that was over the heads of the cherubim something like a sapphire stone, in appearance resembling a throne, appeared above them. And he spoke to the man clothed in linen and said, "Enter between the whirling wheels under the cherubim, and fill your hands with coals of fire from between the cherubim and scatter them over the city. And he entered in my sight."

"Now the cherubim were standing on the right side of the temple when the man entered, and the cloud filled the inner court. Then the glory of the Lord went up from the cherub to the threshold of the temple, and the temple was filled with the brightness of the glory of the Lord. Moreover, the sound of the wings of the cherubim was heard as far as the outer court, like the voice of God Almighty when He speaks."

"And it came about when He commanded the man clothed in linen, saying, "Take fire from between the whirling wheels, from between the cherubim". He entered and stood beside a wheel. Then the cherub stretched out his hand from between the cherubim to the fire which was between the cherubim, took some and put it into the hands of the one clothed in linen, who took it and went out. And the cherubim appeared to have the form of a man's hand under their wings. Then I looked, and behold, four wheels beside the cherubim, one wheel beside each cherub, and the appearance of the wheels was like the gleam of a tarshish stone."

"And as for their appearance, all four of them had the same likeness, as if one wheel were within another wheel. And when they moved they went in any of their four directions without turning as they went: but they followed in the direction which they faced. And their whole body, their backs, their hands, their wings, and the wheels were full of eyes all around, the wheels belonging to all four of them. The wheels were called in my hearing, the whirling wheels. And each one had four faces. The first face was the face of a cherub, the second face was the face of a man, the third the face of a lion and the fourth the face of an eagle."

"Then the cherubim rose up. They are the living beings that I saw by the river Chebar. Now when the cherubim moved, the wheels would go beside them: also when the cherubim lifed up their wings to rise from the ground, the wheels would not turn from beside them. When the cherubim stood still, the wheels would stand still; and when they rose up, the wheels would rise with them. for the spirit of the living beings was in them."

"Then the glory of the Lord departed from the threshold

of the temple and stood over the cherubim. When the cherubim departed, they lifted their wings and rose up from the earth in my sight with the wheels beside them; and they stood still at the entrance of the east gate of the Lord's house. And the glory of the God of Israel hovered over them."

"These were the living beings that I saw beneath the God of Israel by the river Chebar; so I knew that they were cherubim. Each one had four faces and each one four wings, and beneath their wings was the form of human hands. As for the likeness of their faces, they were the same faces whose appearance I had seen by the river Chebar. Each one went straight ahead." (Ezekiel 10: 1-22).

The cherubim were called upon in the garden of Eden to guard the way to the tree of life. (Genesis 3:24). In the Book of Psalms confirmation is given that the cherubim are seated beneath the throne of God . . . "Oh give ear, Shepherd of Israel, Thou who dost lead Joseph like a flock; Thou who art enthroned above the cherubim, shine forth." (Psalms 80:1), and again, "The Lord reigns, let the peoples tremble; he is enthroned above the cherubim, let the earth shake." (Psalms 99:1).

A man from Merseyside, Mr. Phillips, had a glimpse of angels and their singing is something he will remember vividly for the rest of his life. It came about one day when he was walking up the road, minding his own business, and he met Mrs. Rogerson. Now Mrs. Rogerson was an unmistakable character, being elderly and eccentric she always pushed a baby's pram in which she kept bundles of plastic bags, filled with her world-worn possessions. She was a sparky individual and always stopped to share a joke with Mr. Phillips.

He remembers their last meeting clearly. He had been impressed at how well she looked. "I knew she had not been too well, but when I met her she looked the picture of health. I had been a bit down in the dumps and she seemed to sense this. She asked me what was troubling me. Before I had the chance to reply I found myself suddenly whisked to a different sphere. I was trembling with fright at first as I couldn't make out what was happening. I was totally and fully conscious all the time because I distinctly remember thinking to myself that I had somehow been transported from my road to another plane of existence above human understanding. I don't know exactly how I got there, I only know that it was instantaneous. I still had Mrs. Rogerson's question in my mind but I found that I was unable to answer her. My eyes, mind and heart were overcome by the sight of countless angels. It would be impossible to say how many. The most memorable thing about them was their singing which was indescribably beautiful. Such was the intense feeling of happiness that I could hardly catch my breath. The next moment I was standing in the pathway again. I looked round but Mrs. Rogerson had gone.

"This all happened at exactly 3.00 pm as I was on my way to collect my younger sister from school. You can imagine my astonishment when, on reaching the school, I heard the news that Mrs. Rogerson had been found dead in her house at 12 noon that day. I don't know what kind of an effort it was on her part to take me to the next world in this manner, but I will always treasure the experience."

Angels do not always arrive with serene faces playing harps, as Catherine of Co. Armagh will verify. She was out shopping one day and found herself in an area where the local punks congregated. She felt threatened as she walked along and tried not to look at any of the menacing youths who were calling over to her.

"Because I ignored them they started to shout obscenities at me. I was very frightened but tried not to show it. My heart started to thump when I realised they were following me, about six of them. I quickened my pace but within a few seconds I was surrounded. one of them reached out to grab my handbag, but before he got hold of it, another punk rushed forward from behind me and took a swing at the mugger, knocking him to the ground.

"By the way the gang of thugs reacted, I could tell that the youth who had come to my rescue must have been from a rival gang, but to me he could have been one of them since he was dressed in a black studded leather jacket and trousers, and he had a bright pink Mohican hairstyle which stood on end about six inches into blue spikes.

"I was so thankful for his intervention and when the others saw that he meant business they all ran away. I turned to the youth who faced me and gave me the most dazzling smile. I opened my mouth to say "thank you" and he vanished in front of my eyes! I just stood there with my mouth open in utter amazement.

"When I thought about it afterwards once I'd had a chance to get over the shock, I realized that God works in strange ways indeed. He sent me help in the most appropriate way possible to meet the punks on their own level. Ever since that day, I've never again thought of angels as being somewhat soppy insipid creatures, not the way that one delivered his left hook."

An old well-loved hymn to the guardian angels:

> Dear angel ever at my side
> How loving must thou be
> To leave your home in Heaven to guide
> A sinful soul like me

These must be the most comforting and reassuring words that anyone could ever say to a child.

How many times to we feel aware of the positive and wise protection of our own guardian angels? Everyone at some time or other has had that narrow escape, or the distinct impression that something or someone was trying to divert a planned course of action, only to find out later, that had we followed the inner voice's suggestion we would have been better off. In some cases where the silent instruction has been acted upon, serious and even fatal accidents have been avoided. In most of these cases the persons concerned feel that they have been guided out of trouble.

We have all be allocated a guardian angel, as we see from the Book of Psalms, 91:11, "For He will give His angels charge concerning you, to guard you in all your ways. They will bear you up in their hands, lest you strike your foot against a stone."

chapter twenty-two

POSITIVE CONCLUSIONS

Doctors now accept that the human mind can overcome even the most dreadful illnesses. Most cancerous cells can be eliminated by the natural immune systems of the body, but only if the mind allows these defences to work properly. It appears that the 'rogue cell' once thought to be the culprit is not, in itself, the cause of the illness.

The attitude of the person affected plays a dynamic role in recovery. Positive thoughts enlighten the spirit and allow the body to function in a way which is beneficial to the person as a whole. Negative thoughts dampen the spirit and cause disorder in the body mechanisms, including the immune system.

You can use the forces of your mind to assist you with any supposedly unsolvable problem. Just tell your subconscious mind what you wish to achieve and ask it to find the answer. Then forget about it altogether and relax. Lo and behold, a little while later, the answer will pop into your conscious mind and you will think to yourself 'Now why didn't I think of that before.'

Positive loving thoughts create an atmosphere of friendliness and wellbeing. This sets up a chain-reaction of goodwill. Ninety-five people would not have died at Hillsborough in Sheffield on that fateful Saturday if there had been goodwill instead of chaos. Why did people have to die to create the subsequent wonderful scene of camaraderie between Liverpool and Everton fans? Why couldn't it have always been like that?

Most other spectator sports seem to attract people who

share the true spirit of sportsmanship. No trouble at baseball, cricket or rugby games. What is it about the mentality of the minority of football supporters that causes them to spread such havoc?

It only takes a tiny spark of love and goodwill to ignite the imagination of an entire nation to support such good causes as The Great Ormond Street Wishing Well Appeal; Comic Relief and Amnesty International. If we all take an active step to consciously think positive thoughts, the domino effect this would have on mankind would bring stunning changes and untold happiness.

THE CHILDREN THAT TIME FORGOT

"The most unusual book of the year"
– Derek Naylor, Yorkshire Evening Post

Peter and Mary Harrison

WITCHCRAFT CONSPIRACY

CONSPIRACY

Graham St. John-Willey

Watch out for

for

Spinechiller

by
Peter and Mary
Harrison

Published by **Sinclair**

SPRING 1990

The Mystique of Love

BY
PETER & MARY HARRISON

OUT SOON

We are presently researching our next book. If you have seen a ghost, please send your account of the sighting to us at the following address:

PETER & MARY HARRISON
50 OXFORD STREET
WELLINGBOROUGH
NORTHANTS
NN8 4JH